There's no way to describe this book other than brilliant. Every evangelical Christian should read it. It is Christ-like, biblical, pastoral, informed, insightful, compassionate and loving evangelicalism at its best. It is necessary reading if you've got gay friends, and essential reading if you haven't. Buy three, read one and pass the rest on.

Justin Thacker, Head of Theology at Evangelical Alliance

In the Christian world today discussions about homosexuality have inevitably polarized into those who argue that homosexuality should be completely accepted and affirmed, and others who continue to state that homosexual practice is sinful. Caught in the middle, however, are those like Alex, who take the Bible seriously and are seeking to live faithful Christian lives, but who battle with their need for sexual and emotional fulfilment through same-sex bonding.

This book, with its moving stories, is a plea that the wider Christian community, while continuing to endorse the sinfulness of homosexual practice, should have much more understanding of homosexual orientation; that for many this cannot be changed by a quick prayer, but is a journey towards healing from the childhood wounds and misunderstandings which helped cause the condition. It deserves to be read by many Christians, particularly those involved in any sort of pastoral care or healing ministry.

Rachel Tingle, journalist and author

This is a fine book. It contains a wealth of information on the important area of understanding gay people. It shows how one can go beyond superficially accepting such relationships, so as to meet the emotional needs of those struggling with their sexuality. The book points a way forward through such difficulties to enable sound witness.

Jennifer Jones, Christian biblical counsellor, CWR Advice and Referral Service

It's rare these days to find a book on homosexuality that is honest, compassionate and fully aware of the gay experience from the inside, yet equally honest and straightforward about the Bible and unembarrassed to affirm and follow its teaching.

Alex Tylee's book manages this feat with freshness and style. I have no doubt that it will be an enormous help not only to Christians struggling with homosexual experiences and orientation, but especially to their friends and family and churches. The stories and examples dotted throughout are illuminating and encouraging, and there are insightful chapters on how churches could do a better job in reaching out to the gay community, and supporting and helping Christians with a homosexual orientation.

This is a book which joyfully affirms that repentance is part of the good news of the gospel, while recognizing that the path of repentance in our broken and sinful world is rarely smooth and never without cost.

Tony Payne, Publishing Director, Matthias Media, Australia

The rawness Alex conveys in her description of certain circumstances gives the reader the impression she is sneaking a look into the author's most secret journal. Her writing is edgy and unhindered by slick Christian phraseology, allowing the reader to stand with her at the coalface as she grapples with her homosexual orientation and her faith. The chapter entitled 'Identity and Evangelism' is exceptionally powerful and Alex successfully guides the reader into the mindset of a homosexual man or woman. This deeper understanding of an individual and a group of people can only help those friends, family and fellowships who seek to come alongside men and women with a homosexual orientation.

Jeanette Howard, author of Out of Egypt *and* Into the Promised Land

Walking with Gay Friends

Walking with Gay Friends

A journey of informed compassion

Alex Tylee

ivp

INTER-VARSITY PRESS
Norton Street, Nottingham NG7 3HR, England
Email: ivp@ivpbooks.com
Website: www.ivpbooks.com

First published 2007
Reprinted 2010

British Library Cataloguing in Publication Data
A catalogue record for this book is available from the British Library.

ISBN: 978–1–84474–212–7

Set in 10.5/13pt Dante
Typeset in Great Britain by CRB Associates, Potterhanworth, Lincolnshire
Printed in Great Britain by Ashford Colour Press Ltd, Gosport, Hampshire

*Inter-Varsity Press publishes Christian books that are true to the Bible and that
communicate the gospel, develop discipleship and strengthen the church for its
mission in the world.*

*Inter-Varsity Press is closely linked with the Universities and Colleges Christian
Fellowship, a student movement connecting Christian Unions in universities and
colleges throughout Great Britain, and a member movement of the International
Fellowship of Evangelical Students. Website: www.uccf.org.uk*

This book is dedicated to
my parents,with love

Also to Ella,
whose friendship is
the positive example
that inspired this book

Acknowledgment

This book would not have been possible without the help of many friends and colleagues. It's not possible to list you here, but you know who you are. Thank you for your honesty and vulnerability in telling me your stories. Thank you for reading and rereading my drafts, often with unreasonably imposed deadlines on my part. Thanks for your helpful suggestions and encouragements. Thanks for helping me to deal with my ongoing obsession with commas. Thanks for your invaluable and much-needed prayers. Thanks for being the kind of friend that has meant I have been spared much of the painful stuff recounted in this book, but have enjoyed the kind of support that I pray many others will enjoy because of it. My thanks go especially to W. This is so much your story, too.

Author's disclaimer

The quotations used in this book are from actual conversations with real people, most of whom are friends of mine; the others are from relevant organizations or other personal contacts. Most names, including mine, have been changed in order to protect the identities of those involved. Some stories given as examples are amalgamations of my own experiences mixed with those of people I know or that I have witnessed.

Contents

	Foreword	15
1	My story	17
2	What the Bible says	29
3	Origins	43
4	Identity and evangelism	69
5	After conversion	89
6	Wrong reaction, right reaction	113
7	Commissioning	143
	Suggestions for further reading	149
	Notes	151

Foreword

It is a real privilege to write the foreword for Alex's book.

Christians can all too easily live as if there is a hierarchy of sin. We forget that we have all fallen short of the glory God intended us to demonstrate day by day. We do not take into account our sins of omission, or the sins in our hearts; where we have been unforgiving, or impatient, or passive aggressive. So we are vulnerable to judgment and pride. We become confused when we encounter 'live' sin and forget that, before the cross, we stand on a level playing field.

So first, this book reminds us that as none of us is without sin, so none of us is entitled to throw the first stone. The biblical texts around this are well discussed and the conclusions well drawn.

Then, the book clearly lays out the roots of same-sex attraction, avoiding the pitfall of any formula and reassuring us that there are logical reasons why our unmet needs may become eroticized and cry out for expression in this way.

The use of personal testimony gives this book vitality and authority. It is timely both for the debates and the pastoral dilemmas within the church family, and for navigating personal friendships as Christ would want.

I believe this book will enable those for whom same-sex attraction is an issue to dare to hope for more and for change; and bring a refreshing and informed compassion to those who journey with them.

Dr Lisa Guinness
Director of the Living Waters Discipleship and Healing Trust

My story

I guess initially I had always assumed I was a Christian. My parents were churchgoers, I had been christened as a baby, I owned a Bible and I was a nice person. Religion wasn't something that I gave much thought to; it was just a nice background thing that was part of being middle-class and English. I didn't see it as something big enough to conflict with my increasingly evident homosexual feelings.

As I look back on childhood, I can identify some things that made me a bit different. I can remember, at primary school, being asked what I would like to be when I grew up. I said that I would like to be a policeman. 'Don't you mean a policewoman?' the teacher laughed. I was confused, because in my head I had imagined myself as an adult man. I felt much more like a little boy than a little girl.

Moving on to middle and secondary school, I can remember having certain female friends whom I would put on pedestals. These girls occupied so much of my thinking that I hardly noticed as my other friends began to fight for the attentions of boys, who for me were too irrelevant even to appear on my radar. By seventeen, I remember a particular attraction to one girl who shared two of my subjects at A level. She was creative, intelligent and popular in a way that for me made her stand out amongst my peers. I took a great interest in her ideas, thoughts and emotions and began to realize that my feelings for her were more than just a special interest; they were developing into feelings of physical and sexual attraction. One evening when my parents were out, I remember watching a programme on TV about lesbians. I found that I could relate so much to the feelings these women were describing that I had to admit to myself explicitly, for the first time, that I was gay.

... it seemed incredibly unreasonable that I should be condemned for something that was just a natural part of me.

Around the same time as I was dealing with this, I can remember looking through my Gideon Bible, which I had been given for free at school. I looked down the list of topics entitled 'Where to find help in times of need' and was intrigued to find the heading 'Sexual immorality'. I flicked to it, in the manner of a teenager looking up naughty words in the dictionary, and found the phrase 'homosexual offenders' (1 Corinthians 6:9). *Offenders?* The phrase seemed so outdated and bigoted. I really could not believe that any God would say a thing like that. I knew that I had not chosen my sexuality, so it seemed incredibly unreasonable that I should be condemned for something that was just a natural part of me. I concluded that the Bible must have been written by some homophobic bigots thousands of years ago and was not a document to be taken seriously. I decided that I was not a Christian after all, which was no great loss to me, as it had made no impact on my life in the first place.

I did not think about God again until I went to university. One of the first people I met when I enrolled on my course happened to be a Christian. I had never come across a Christian like this before. For her, her belief in God seemed actually to affect her life. She regularly read the Bible and even believed that it was the inspired word of God. What puzzled me even more was that I liked her; she was clever, fun and down to earth. I found it hard to reconcile the two: an intelligent person whom I respected, and yet someone who believed something as ridiculous and outdated as Christianity.

Over the next two years, we had several conversations about her beliefs. I found it fascinating that she seemed so unashamed to admit to being a Christian. She used to take me along to evangelistic meetings that the Christian Union put on, and I would politely make comments like 'very interesting', having dismissed all that I had heard.

I was shocked to hear that being nice and owning a Bible did not give me an automatic ticket to eternal life.

However, I can remember one or two talks that struck a chord. One was about Jesus, called 'Jesus: Mad, Bad or God?' Jesus' life did not seem to point to the conclusion that he was mad or evil. As he appeared in the Bible, he seemed so loving and coherent. He claimed to be God and he did all kinds of amazing things, which were recorded by *secular* historians as well as Gospel writers and which, if they were true, would back up that claim. I couldn't quite explain Jesus away. If, as the speaker claimed, the Gospels were historically reliable documents, then who was this man? If he *was* God, I really ought to take him seriously. Another talk was called 'Am I Good Enough for Heaven?' I was shocked to hear at this talk that being nice and owning a Bible did not give me an automatic ticket to eternal life. I was not sure whether I believed in an afterlife, but I did not like the idea that if there was one, I'd be excluded. However, I had not forgotten what I had found in my Gideon Bible a few years before. I knew I did not want to become a Christian. In fact, I guess I thought I was automatically excluded because of my sexuality. I pushed all of these thoughts aside and carried on living as I had before.

I hadn't yet told many people that I was gay, and I certainly did not want to tell my Christian friend; I felt that it would risk our friendship, because of what she believed. However, one afternoon she told me that she wanted to have a chat with me about something. I could see that she meant it to be a serious chat, so I agreed to meet her, wondering what she might say. She told me that she knew that I was gay and that she wanted me to know that it was something that we could talk about together, if I wanted to. I was really thrilled because my fears of rejection had not been realized. I felt accepted.

However, the next few days of openness between my friend and me were not what I had hoped. Whenever I began talking about my future hopes for relationships, she looked uncomfortable. I decided it was time for another 'chat'. I confronted her and she explained that, although she was my friend and accepted me as I was, she could not condone me having a relationship, because she believed that the Bible said that it was wrong and she could not compromise on it. She explained that the Bible said that homosexual *conduct* was wrong, not a homosexual inclination. She could accept and love me just as I was, but she could not with a clear conscience encourage me to find a girlfriend. She went on to tell me that, whether I was straight or gay, I was living in a way that did not please God, because I was not acknowledging him with my life. She basically told me, in as loving a way as she could, that the alternative to becoming a Christian was hell.

Our friendship was on shaky ground for the next few days, because I was really angry and offended by what she had said to me. I could not believe that she was making these judgmental comments about my life, and that she had the audacity to tell me that I deserved hell. Underneath all of this was the nagging fear that she might be right. I had not forgotten what I had heard in those talks from the Christian Union. I knew that if this man Jesus *was* God, then I had to listen to what he said, and I knew that he said that hell was my destination unless I accepted him as my saviour. But celibacy? I was nineteen years old! I didn't even want to consider such a possibility, so I squashed all thoughts of God for another year.

During that time I began to feel a little more confident in my sexuality. I began to come out to a few more friends and went to a few gay and lesbian events put on by my university. When I was with other gay people I really felt as if I had come home. I felt at last that I had found a place where I could be accepted and feel that I could be myself. After a lifetime of feeling different, I had found 'my people'. I found the gay scene welcoming, liberating and exciting.

> *I knew that if this man Jesus was God, then I had to listen to what he said.*

I had been happily avoiding my friend's invitations to Christian Union events all year, but in my final year the CU put on a week of lunchtime evangelistic talks. She nagged and nagged, until I found myself listening to the first four. Each one knocked down another of my carefully constructed arguments against Christianity, until there was only one talk left. It was called 'Jesus: No One Forgets a Good Teacher?' I was nervous about this one, because I knew that Jesus was the only thing left that I had not been able to explain away. I was still troubled by the thought of this man who claimed to be God.

The talk was based on Mark chapter 2, which documents a time when Jesus is presented with a paralysed man who wants to be healed. Jesus shocks the crowd by telling the man that his sins are forgiven. Only after this does he heal him, to prove to the cynics that he is able, and that he does have the authority to forgive sins; authority that belongs to God alone. The speaker explained that the paralysed man really *wanted* to be healed. But Jesus saw his greater need, which was to be forgiven. The speaker said to us all that we might have things that we really *wanted* in this life, but that we had a need which was greater. We needed forgiveness from God.

I had a decision to make. By now, I knew that Jesus *was* who he claimed to be. Who else could he be but God? I also knew what a sacrifice it would mean for me to say no to ever having a relationship with a woman, and to deny this identity that had seemed to bring me such liberty. But what was my alternative? If Jesus was God, then he was ruler of the world. I had no choice but to submit to him. I went to my room and with many tears asked Jesus to forgive me, fully believing that I was throwing my life away and that this was day one of a long and lonely wait for heaven. In my first believing prayer, I told God that he had better expect failure, because I was far weaker than he knew. After praying I opened up my Bible and found Psalm 34. The words seemed to shout directly at me, and I knew that God was replying to my prayer through them:

> *Jesus saw his greater need, which was to be forgiven.*

The eyes of the LORD are on the righteous
  and his ears are attentive to their cry . . .
The righteous cry out, and the LORD hears them;
  he delivers them from all their troubles.
The LORD is close to the broken-hearted
  and saves those who are crushed in spirit.

A righteous man may have many troubles,
    but the LORD delivers him from them all.
(Psalm 34:15, 17–19)

I knew then that God had heard my prayer and answered. He was telling me that, yes, the path ahead of me was going to be a tough one, but that he would hear and help me every time I cried out to him. He would be walking this journey with me.

It is now several years since that day. Being honest, I would say that the first two or three were probably the hardest of my life. All of my hopes and ambitions for the future had been based upon settling down and being happy and in love with someone. It was incredibly difficult to adjust to the prospect of a life of singleness and celibacy. I had no idea yet of what God was like, so any concept of healing, or change in my orientation, was alien to me. I was acutely aware of my sexuality, and its pull away from God was incredibly strong at times. I was also fairly isolated, as I felt very different from other Christians, finding it hard to be open with them and so avoiding investing in close friendships.

It was incredibly difficult to adjust to the prospect of a life of singleness and celibacy.

    Around two years after my conversion, I met a woman at work who was clearly and openly gay. I was quickly fascinated by this woman, who showed such pride in this thing that I was still quite afraid of. I felt liberated when I was around her, and proud of the things that normally made me feel shame. It was not long before my fascination turned to obsession, our friendship became increasingly close and we fell in love. We had a brief sexual relationship, which ended as quickly as it began, mainly because I still believed that it was wrong to have a homosexual relationship. We agreed, with immense pain, never to see each other again. It was as I tried to start again, to recover from this relationship that had turned my world upside down, that I was forced to run further into the arms of God. It was through this that I finally began to understand more of the gospel of grace and so began to rejoice in my status as a child of God. Slowly I understood that grace meant that I was no more or less sinful than any other Christian. I understood that Christ died for me personally, as well as for the world, that he had created me uniquely and that I was precious to him. I began to learn what it means to be a part of the Christian family, and that this could be a *real* family that could ease my aloneness and to which I could contribute with the gifts that God had given me.

Slowly I understood that grace meant that I was no more or less sinful than any other Christian.

Of course, none of this meant that living in a way that was pleasing to God stopped being a struggle. Four years on another friendship became physical, and I have recently had to end still another because of increasingly inappropriate emotional closeness and a strong mutual attraction. Losing friends in this way never gets any easier; it is certainly where my battle with sin has its highest cost. Positively, I have begun to see changes: I have begun to learn to relate healthily to men as friends instead of avoiding them, and to have more friendships with women that do not become sexualized.

As I continue to try to live the life of a celibate gay Christian, I feel I can relate a lot to Noah when he was building the ark. There must have been numerous times while he was building an enormous boat in the middle of a parched desert when he wondered if he was being a complete fool. I have no doubt that plenty of people laughed at him, probably to his face. He must have been tempted as he looked around him, seeing no evidence of any logic to what he was doing, to think that they were the ones with sense. He must have wondered whether God really knew what he was doing, or if he was playing a sick joke on him, or if he could be trusted. He must have been tempted to lay down his hammer and stop the hard physical slog and eat, drink and be merry with everyone else.

As I continue to say no to perfectly lovely girls and to live with sporadic bouts of loneliness, while others seem to enjoy happiness in gay relationships all over the world and right under my nose, I find myself asking similar questions. Even some of the people closest to me in my life seem to think I am some kind of masochist. In my most difficult times, I feel inclined to agree with them. I feel like a loony saying no to love and yes to loneliness. It does look like madness and masochism from the outside. I often wonder whether God really knows what he is doing in saying that this is the way that I should live, or if he is playing a sick joke on me, or if he can be trusted. I am often tempted to lay down the hammer of holiness and stop this hard slog, giving in like so many of the people around me.

In the midst of all of my struggles, the truth is that I serve a Lord who loves me and who loves to bless me.

But Noah was proved right in his apparent madness. The flood did come, and on that day I bet he was more than glad that he had put up with the ridicule and carried on trusting through his doubts. I need to hold on tight to the truth that there will come a day when I will see that it was right to be obedient. That the painful cost of every romantic relationship that I have ended or never begun has been worthwhile. That though, each time, it felt and looked like madness, there will come a day when it will become clear why the Lord has asked me to live this way, and I will wish I had said no more often.

Having walked this path for several years now, I have failed more profoundly than I imagined I could, but also seen some of that authentic joy that only a Christian can have, because it comes straight from heaven. In the midst of all of my struggles, the truth is that I serve a Lord who loves me and who loves to bless me. Jesus died on the cross for all the ugly manifestations of my sexuality struggles, as much as he did for any other sin; this gives me hope, as I strive on, that 'he who began a good work in [me] will carry it on to completion until the day of Christ Jesus' (Philippians 1:6). The same Jesus who would not leave my mind, however hard I tried to push him out, has now become my friend, my Lord and my brother. He *is* a Beautiful Saviour. I *love* my Lord, and I love knowing him, walking alongside him and sharing him with others. I have a reason for living, which is for his glory, and I have a sure and perfect future ahead of me in heaven. I have eternal value and I live according to the truth revealed by the maker of the universe. Who would not be a Christian? At whatever cost, who would choose anything else?

I have eternal value and I live according to the truth revealed by the maker of the universe.

I am often asked whether I hope for God to 'heal' me and lead me into marriage. For most of my Christian life my sexuality has still been so much a part of my identity that I have not wanted to change, even though it was such a source of struggle in my walk with God. I was also too sceptical in the beginning to believe that God really *could* change something so apparently fundamental in me, even if I had wanted him to. As I have lived longer as a

Christian and witnessed God doing all kinds of modern miracles in my own life and those of my friends, I am much more inclined to believe that I serve a God who most certainly could change my sexual orientation enough for me to have as happy and godly a marriage as anyone.

However, there is a cost to be borne in praying that kind of prayer – the risk of daring to hope. It is frightening to make oneself willing to co-operate with God in the process by which such a specific sanctification might come about; a process which would inevitably be painful and probably long. What if I were to let God into such a wounded, private and fundamental part of me – to let him pull it apart and put it back together again – and still did not regain that dream of love and companionship that I had first had to grieve over losing at my conversion? Thus far, it has seemed easier to accept the pain of grieving that loss rather than risk the potentially greater pain of taking it up again, only to have it taken away in a different form in the future if – as for many healthy heterosexuals – marriage still does not happen for me.

... he will be sufficient whatever my future holds ...

Recently, however, I have felt challenged in this fear. Challenged in that, for me at least, there is a certain disobedience in not trusting God with this: that he will be sufficient whatever my future holds, and that he has every right to deal with every wounded bit of my heart should he so choose, whatever the consequences. I have just begun to take the first tentative steps in letting God in to that part of my heart, praying that the hope of marriage or heterosexuality would never become just a different kind of idol. Nor do I want to put unrealistic expectations on the hope that marriage or heterosexuality would diminish my loneliness, selfishness or battle with sin. These are very real dangers, and I am under no illusions that being capable of heterosexual sin would make me any more godly than being susceptible to homosexual sin. There is a delicate balance to be held between opening up such a door of hope and maintaining the discipline of seeking to be content in all circumstances, even lifelong singleness; something that I do not want to compromise in any way.

Meanwhile, for those of us who are trying to live a life of sexual abstinence as we struggle with homosexual feelings, it often feels like being on the front line of the battle. The controversy over homosexuality is rarely out of the media and provokes strong feeling from every camp. Putting our money where our mouths are by trying to live this out is a provocative statement in itself; we are visibly taking up a costly cross without even opening our mouths, and one that will inevitably be viewed by some as condemnatory. The front line is a dangerous place to be in any battle; people like me need all the help and support that we can get.

Whenever I share my own story, I come across Christians who tell me about friends they have who need help. Some have a gay non-Christian friend with whom they long to share the gospel, but do not know where to start or how best to be sensitive. Others have Christian friends who are struggling with their sexuality. They want to help them and love them well, but they do not know where to begin: the friends' struggles can seem on the surface so complicated and so different from their own. I chose to write this book to help those people to love their friends with informed compassion: to see how we can work together as the body of Christ to witness to non-Christian homosexuals; and to support Christians who have this particular struggle. We will also see that we have plenty in common; we are running the same race with the same Saviour cheering us on.

What the Bible says

Andy says:

I first faced up to the challenge of what the Bible said
when I was a Christian and in a relationship with a bloke.
But it was more a response to the conviction that the
relationship was wrong rather than a conviction that what
the Bible said was right. My head was messed up by how I
felt about the guy that I loved and how I felt about Jesus,
who I knew loved me in a more profound way. I made a
choice to end the relationship on the conviction that it was
wrong – but I wanted to keep the relationship; I wanted
the Bible to say that it was OK.[1]

As homosexual practice becomes more and more acceptable in
society, the debate has raged ever more bitterly about what the
Bible really says about the subject of homosexuality. Both sides
appear to have convincing arguments, even referring back to the
original Greek and Hebrew to give credence to their views. It can
be very confusing for someone wishing to show Christian love and

understanding to a person struggling with homosexual feelings, when both sides can seem so convincing.

As a non-Christian, when I had first heard the gospel but was not yet convinced that it was true, I wanted to find out what Christians really thought about the homosexuality issue. I was faced with a confusing array of materials. There are Christian organizations such as LGCM (the Lesbian & Gay Christian Movement), whose statement of conviction includes the line 'it is entirely compatible with the Christian faith not only to love another person of the same sex but also to express that love fully in a personal sexual relationship'. There are also organizations such as TFT (True Freedom Trust), one clause of whose basis of faith reads: 'Our understanding of Bible teaching is that, although many people may be aware of homosexual or lesbian feelings, homosexual genital conduct falls short of God's plan for his Creation.'

When we look at what the Bible says about sexuality as a whole, it becomes clearer that the passages on homosexuality are unambiguous and entirely consistent.

Which viewpoint is right? It's essential that we start from God's perspective. When we look at what the Bible says about sexuality as a whole, it becomes clearer that the passages on homosexuality are unambiguous and entirely consistent. It's also important to start here, so that when we are saying that homosexual conduct is wrong, we can be sure that our answers are *biblical* and not simply based on sociological or medical reasons, or on personal viewpoint. Many Christians will confidently say that homosexual conduct is wrong, but far fewer are able to back this up with biblical evidence rather than subjective opinion. So in this chapter I want to give a summary of the debate: to give an overview of what the Bible *really* says on the subject.[2]

I shall start by thinking about how Christians should treat the Bible in general. It is a book that needs to be handled carefully, because it has many authors. It was written, over a period of thousands of years that ended almost 2,000 years ago, by men who lived in cultures very different from the one we live in now. This means that interpreting it in the context of today's culture is often difficult.

On the other hand, Christians believe that the Bible is God's word; that everything contained in it is God's revelation to us. For that reason we place enormous importance on everything contained in it.

Context

So when Christians read the Bible today they must first understand what the author meant at the time, and only then decide how to apply those principles today. It is sometimes hard to do this, but if we believe that God is the Bible's ultimate author, then the morality in it will be as constant and unchanging as he is: not something to be 'updated' as society changes, but funda- mentals relevant for all time. It

... when Christians read the Bible today they must first understand what the author meant at the time ...

is our responsibility to take into account the intended meaning of the Bible's authors, removing the clothing of culture, language and personal bias and getting to the core biblical truth. The best way of knowing that we have achieved this with our text is to see whether it fits in with the rest of the Bible. Correct biblical interpretation is not always easy or straightforward, but is not impossible either. We have a responsibility to resist the temptation to make the Bible say what we wish it said, or to listen for what our 'itching ears want to hear' (2 Timothy 4:3). It takes courage to hear the truth.

Those who argue in favour of homosexual conduct focus on detailed reinterpretations of the specific texts that mention it. There is not sufficient space here to examine each of these; here I will be giving only a brief overview of what the Bible says about homosexual conduct. The 'Further reading' section at the end of the book will help those who wish to study this in more detail. The first thing to do here is to look at what the Bible as a whole affirms about sexuality in general, and then at why homosexual conduct does not fit into this picture.

Positive sexuality[3]

Right from Genesis to Revelation, the Bible affirms the union of one man with one woman for life within marriage as God's ideal and sole intended outlet for the expression of human sexuality. Read the first two chapters of Genesis. They describe the world when God first created it, with everything as he intended it to be. Notice how many times God declares something to be 'good'. It is clear that God was pleased with his creation as it was then. Look in particular at chapter 1, verse 27, 'male and female he created them', and then at verse 31: 'God saw all that he had made and it was very good.' It is obvious here that God created a man and a woman, and that he was pleased that he had done so. So what? Why should we take this seriously in our study of biblical sexuality? Three reasons.

God's creation of man and woman as complementary partners occurred while everything was still as God intended.

Firstly, the fact that this passage is not strictly a 'moral lesson' in the way that, say, parts of Paul's letters are does not mean that we are not to take it seriously. The Bible reveals truth in many different ways, of which story form is just one. If we ignored this passage for that reason, we would be forced to ignore a large proportion of the rest of the Bible too.

Secondly, it is hugely significant that these descriptions take place before the 'fall' or rebellion in chapter 3. Genesis 3 (and the rest of the Bible) shows us that everything that is right with the world is in the first two chapters: the world as God intended it. Everything that is wrong with it is seen from chapter 3 onwards: the world spoilt by man's rebellion against God. God's creation of man and woman as complementary partners occurred while everything was still as God intended.

Thirdly, this passage is consistent with what the rest of the Bible says about sexuality. This is important. Where we find consistency, we know we are getting to the truth. Jesus and Paul both quote directly from here when talking about sexuality and marriage (see Matthew 19:3–8 and 1 Corinthians 6:12–20). Genesis 1 and 2 are a really important foundation for a study of biblical sexuality. Here are some other important things we can take from this passage:

- Reproduction is good: Genesis 1:28, affirmed in 17:2 and in Psalm 127:3.
- Sex is good: Genesis 2:23–25, affirmed in the Song of Songs and in 1 Corinthians 7:4–5.
- Marriage is good: implied in Genesis; assumed throughout the Old Testament; and affirmed by Jesus in Matthew 19:3–8 and by Paul in 1 Corinthians 6 – 7.
- Male and female are necessary counterparts: Genesis 1:27 (that's how we were created to be) and 2:18 and 2:23 – the union of the two corresponding sexes is 'good'. She is his companion (2:18) and they are physically fitting (2:23–24).

So it is clear that all of this is 'good' in the eyes of God. So far, either directly from the passages mentioned, or by implication from them, we can ascertain that heterosexual union is good, first because only this union produces children. This is good because the children are able to learn from both sexes, thus developing their own sexuality in a healthy way.

Secondly, it is good because only heterosexual union joins two fully complementary people. Genesis gives us insight into the fact that God designed men and women as two different, but complementary, types that must go together. Physically, this is obvious: the penis fits inside the vagina, and the fit is designed to be pleasurable. Homosexual sex can only ever be a simulation or substitute for this. The Bible demands that we honour God by using our bodies in the way that he intended them to be used (see Romans 12:1 and 1 Corinthians 6:20). It is true that homosexuals often manage very well to give one another pleasure without the genitals of the opposite sex being present, but it is important to remember that nothing on this earth was given us only for our own pleasure. In all things we should seek to honour and glorify God; to do that with our sexuality, we must use it in the way that God clearly intended.

The Bible demands that we honour God by using our bodies in the way that he intended them to be used.

Profound mystery

It is also worth pointing out that Paul refers to the Genesis account of one-flesh union (2:24) in Ephesians 5:31, saying this in the following verse: 'This is a profound mystery, but I am talking about Christ and the church.' There is a spiritual dimension to heterosexual marriage. It is a reflection of the relationship between Christ and the church. There are several passages in the Old and New Testament that back this up, as the analogy of husband and wife is used again and again when describing the relationship between God and Israel (Ezekiel 16:6–14 is one example). Israel is often denounced as an unfaithful wife: for instance, in Ezekiel 23 and in the book of Hosea. In the New Testament, too, we find Jesus describing himself as the bridegroom and the church as his bride (for example, in Mark 2:19–20). All this is significant, since any deviation from this must be a distortion of that 'profound mystery', this earthly illustration of God's relationship with us. Adultery illustrates the idolatry of Israel in Ezekiel 23 and Hosea. Masturbation, pornography and same-sex unions show a church seeking only itself, not God. They are distortions of the God-given picture of Christ and the church in Ephesians 5.

So that is a summary of what the Bible has to say about sexuality in general. This by itself excludes our taking a positive view of homosexual conduct. There are also, however, a few texts that specifically address this subject.

Old Testament

There are several mentions of homosexual conduct in the Old Testament, some more useful than others in trying to achieve a biblical overview. Two that are often mentioned are Leviticus 18:22 and 20:13. There are

Adultery illustrates the idolatry of Israel in Ezekiel 23 and Hosea.

other verses in the Old Testament that mention homosexual conduct, such as those in Genesis (19:1–8) and Judges (19:16–30), but it is difficult to use them on their own as texts to make a particular point about it. Each of these references has inspired much debate and would need a large amount of space to do justice to the complexities of the arguments involved. However, it is not strictly necessary to be familiar with these debates to have a broad understanding of how Christians should understand homosexual conduct in the Bible. There is enough in the New Testament, when read in the context of human sexuality as a whole, to lead us to a solid conclusion. For this reason I have chosen not to look at the Old Testament passages in detail here.[4]

New Testament
Romans

There are a couple of main texts in the New Testament that mention homosexual conduct specifically. The first is Romans 1:26–27. This is an unambiguous condemnation of homosexual conduct among both men and women. However, it is important to note the context. The mention of homosexual conduct comes among a list of a whole spectrum of human failings, from gossip to murder. Paul is making the broader point that all of humanity has naturally 'exchanged the truth of God for a lie' (verse 25). The result is that God 'gives us over' to what we desire. In other words, as we reject God, we get what we ask for; he allows us to indulge in our rebellion and reap the consequences. One result of this is that sexuality becomes distorted. Humans choose to use it to satisfy themselves, rather than to glorify God in its right context of marriage. One such distortion is homosexual conduct. However, there is no hierarchy of sin in this passage. The homosexual sin is not written in red ink, or, as one person expressed it imaginatively, the pinnacle of some literary palindrome. It is one sin among a list from which we can all find ourselves guilty of something, as Paul drives home in 2:1: 'You, therefore, have no excuse.'

Humans choose to use sexuality to satisfy themselves, rather than to glorify God in its right context of marriage.

'Naturally', we would be in our pre-fall state, living lives in harmony with God and one another, and enjoying the gift of sexuality as God intended it in Genesis 1 and 2. But our individual and corporate rebellion since Genesis 3 means that we have chosen – and God has given us over to – what is 'unnatural' to our original created state. This applies to all the sins that Paul lists, as well as those that he omits.

1 Corinthians
The second key New Testament text, 1 Corinthians 6:9–11, similarly gives a list of sinful behaviours which are not compatible with membership of God's kingdom:

Do you not know that the wicked will not inherit the kingdom of God? Do not be deceived: Neither the sexually immoral nor idolaters nor adulterers nor male prostitutes nor homosexual offenders nor thieves nor the greedy nor drunkards nor slanderers nor swindlers will inherit the kingdom of God. And that is what some of you were. But you were washed, you were sanctified, you were justified in the name of the Lord Jesus Christ and by the Spirit of our God.

. . . all Christians have been washed, sanctified and justified, once and for all time, by the blood of Jesus.

'Homosexual offenders' (the Greek here referring to male homosexual conduct) are listed among adulterers, drunkards and thieves. Paul's main point in this passage comes in the gloriously hope-filled words of verse 11: 'And that is what some of you *were*.' Though Christians may continue to struggle with the tempt-ation to steal, or to have sex with someone who is not their marriage partner, the fact is that all Christians have *been* washed, sanctified and justified, once and for all time, by the blood of Jesus. The penalty for homosexual sin, and all other sin, has been comprehensively paid by Jesus for all those who trust in him. Nevertheless, it is clear that homosexual conduct is no more appropriate in the lifestyle of a Christian than prostitution or adultery.

'If it feels good, do it'?

Having looked at what the Bible has to say, the broad principles to understand are that God created our sexuality to be used within the confines of heterosexual monogamy within marriage. Any expression of sexuality outside this undermines it and cannot glorify God. Even if one of the revisionist arguments which are positive about homosexual conduct seems to make sense on its own, it cannot stand alone in the light of biblical sexual theology as a whole. Having examined in detail the implausibility of liberal biblical argument, the only argument that remains is that it feels good to the individuals involved. This attitude has no place within Christian morality and, when taken to its logical conclusion, can include paedophilia, bestiality (sex with animals) and incest, so long as the experience is positive for those involved.

As representatives of God, we are to have high and holy standards too, sexually as well as in every other area.

It is worth saying that in the real world gay relationships can and often do work. There are of course some happy and apparently healthy relationships in existence between two people of the same sex. When God calls Christians to be different, it is not always because the world's alternative 'doesn't work'. Christians struggling with their sexuality who live by this premise will quickly come unstuck if they should find themselves involved with someone of the same sex, because they may well find contentment and happiness in these 'sinful' relationships and then use this experience to discount God's word.

Living distinctive and separate lives for God is never just about having good experiences or feelings. Most sin feels good; or else we would not be tempted to sin. God is holy, in the purest imaginable sense of the word. That means that his standards are high. As representatives of God, we are to have high and holy standards too, sexually as well as in every other area. This means using our sexuality in the way that God intended. We can use it to worship ourselves, or we can use it to glorify God.

Real world, real people

Everything that I have said from the start of this chapter is abstract. The arguments are convincing, but people are not abstractions. People have feelings and are left fighting against desires and instincts that feel so natural. It is all very well for Christians with homosexual desires to be able to argue a point of view and to understand in their heads why such conduct is wrong. But this does not stop it feeling 'right'; it does not prevent them from wanting it more than anything else; and it does not stop them feeling as if, as Christians, they have drawn the short straw. For a Christian with a homosexual inclination to live a lifestyle of sexual abstinence is hard. But Christians do not have to face anything alone. The Bible does not flinch from saying that being a Christian is hard. It says that if we are to share in Christ's glory, we have to share in his sufferings too. (Look at the parable of the rich young man in Mark 10 and apply this to the struggle of a person with homosexuality issues).

It is important to remember that God is *always* good and that he loves us enough to give his only Son to die the death that we deserve. A God like this can never be seen as a cosmic spoilsport, and this applies also in the case of the Christian struggling with homosexuality. In this context it is clear that the call for sexual abstinence is for the good of both the Christian and the community; God's instructions are never arbitrary. Christians struggling with the reality of this must remember that when they reach heaven, what they suffer now will seem to have been only momentary in the context of eternity. God's wisdom will be theirs, and they will know fully why this was the path God asked them to take.

Until then, we can remind them that, as well as affirming heterosexual monogamy, the Bible also positively affirms singleness. Far from viewing singleness as a 'second-best' option, Paul says he wishes to spare us from the 'many troubles' of marriage. Look at 1 Corinthians 7:27–28. There are many great gifts to be found in marriage, but there are also a lot of hardships. There are many hardships in being single, for sure, but there are also a lot of great gifts to be found. Take the example of our Lord Jesus. He was tempted as we are (Hebrews 4:15), but he chose not to marry. He was not a second-rate human being because he was not sexually active. He led a life rich in relationships of all kinds. Genesis 2:18 says, 'It is not good for the man to be alone.' That is true; God did not intend that any of us should be alone. But singleness is not the same thing as aloneness. God provides companionship in so many rich ways, and Christian companionship can be richer than any other. It is an example to the world.

Far from viewing singleness as a 'second-best' option, Paul says he wishes to spare us from the 'many troubles' of marriage.

Friendship is devalued in contemporary culture. It is often seen as something secondary, or as something to be enjoyed in youth and then largely set aside when marriage takes over. Because of this, most people do not realize the true potential of friendship. We are all so busy searching for intimacy with a lover or partner that we fail to see the rich potential for intimacy in friendship.

If given the time and energy to develop, a friendship can offer companionship, joy, intimacy, openness, vulnerability, physical affection, trust, commitment and safety. It takes effort and vulnerability to allow a friendship like this to develop, but the rewards are amazing and lifelong, and we are allowed as many as we like! Friendship is the currency of life, and we each have the potential to be very rich indeed.

We are human, and it is easy to feel that we need security and affirmation. We do need that – and God has given it to us. As Christians, our past is secure and affirmed because our sins have been forgiven. Our present is secure and affirmed because, even though we continue to sin, we are still forgiven and we have a real hope for the future which nothing can take away (Romans 5:1–11). Our future is secure and affirmed because all our future sins will be forgiven; we will be given new and perfect resurrection bodies when we will live for eternity in the Father's care; and we will know his love completely, which will be more wonderful than we can begin to imagine (Revelation 21). We have been raised with Christ – we do not need anything else.

Friendship is the currency of life, and we each have the potential to be very rich indeed.

God has given us everything that we need to persevere in the meantime. We have his word (but take Hebrews 3:15 to heart), which instructs us, comforts us and shows us our sure hope and promise. We have one another (Hebrews 3:13), to build one another up, encourage, rebuke, praise, and enjoy friendships. And we have Jesus (Hebrews 4:14–16). In our time of need, we can approach him with confidence through grace, and we know that he understands and sympathizes with the cries of our hearts, because he has been fully human too.

Though the Bible contains many things that we find difficult to live out, it also contains much to comfort us. The bottom line is that, whether reading it brings us joy or struggle, it is the true revelation of God. Andy describes how he wrestled with the text in the face of his homosexual feelings.

I read the full gamut of material on different approaches to law, translation, interpretation and application of the biblical texts. Even though I wanted to agree with the liberal side of the debate – I wanted to be able to say that the Bible's authority did not say that loving gay relationships were wrong – I couldn't. It is as clear as day: what the Bible says is that any sex outside of marriage is wrong, because it is a rejection of God's plan for sex. This includes every sexual act, no matter how loving; this constraint applies to everyone and everything. There is no caveat given that would encourage or enable us to consider those who face homosexual orientation to be outside of that all-encompassing moral restriction.

I saw that the choice was either to accept the Bible's authority or to reject it. The option to mess around with the Bible and to make it say what I wanted was simply not open to me; I wanted to live with integrity. This was the crucial choice. I knew that I didn't have the authority to tell God how I should live. The choice was a great cost, but it was the right one: I chose to trust the Bible as God's word.

Origins

Ruth says:

I was only about three when I first remember being aware
that I was attracted to other girls. So it was hard to
remember how I felt, because I suppose it just felt quite
normal and natural because it's what I grew up with. It
wasn't until I started to realize that that wasn't the ordinary
way of things that it probably started to cause me problems
... I suppose I realized I was different when I was at
secondary school; around thirteen or fourteen, when people
are starting to get boyfriends and things like that. I think that
was probably when I thought that this wasn't a phase that
I was going through or a normal stage of my development,
but that in actual fact, I seemed to be quite different from
other people and that seemed to be a lasting thing.[1]

Why do I need to know why?

Is homosexuality a choice, or are people born that way? Does it
go away when a person begins a new life as a Christian? Can
homosexuality[2] be 'healed'?

It's important to know the answers to some of these questions if we want to have realistic expectations and hopes for our gay friends. Christians often hear comparatively little teaching on the subject and so are unclear about how to marry what the Bible says with the reality of the gay people around them, in the media or in their lives.

It's also important for the homosexual struggler, who, on finding at conversion that their feelings have not been magically washed away, may find themselves questioning God as to why he made them this way, or lose all hope of change.

An understanding of the roots of homosexual feelings can begin to bring hope and clarity into all these situations, and will help those seeking to minister to the homosexual struggler to have informed compassion.

Is homosexuality a choice, or are people born that way?

Much has been made in some Christian writings[3] on the subject of the physical and health risks involved in engaging in male homosexual conduct. The statistics surrounding this cannot be denied.[4] It is important to remember that these risks are genuine, and that not all aspects of the gay scene are about 'nice' monogamous relationships between two people who love each other. It must be acknowledged that there is a 'dark side' to the gay scene, permeated by heavy drug use and shocking promiscuity. We do need to be mindful of this to some extent as we witness to this community, because the risks associated with it are real enough to spur on our evangelism even more.

However, I am not going to dwell on this in detail. I am uncomfortable with the fascination that some Christians seem to have in reporting in detail what exactly homosexual men get up to in bed and all the reasons why this perverts God's use of the male body. As I made clear in Chapter 1, I agree that God designed the human body for heterosexual sex, but I feel there are dangers in spending time exploring this in detail. One is that the message often conveyed by such dissection is that this is the reason why God says that gay sex is wrong.

I can remember one such occasion, soon after my conversion, when I had come out to an older Christian, hoping for some compassion and support. He explained in detail how gay sex was wrong because the anus was not designed to receive, only to expel. As if this was relevant to me!

It is important not to lose our focus that our reasoning for saying that homosexual conduct is wrong must come from the fact that God has one context for sexual expression, into which homosexual conduct does not fit. Moreover, a Christian who has been convinced by the 'wrongness' of homosexual conduct based on these scary statistics will then come unstuck when faced with a 'nice' monogamous male partnership or a pair of faithful lesbians. We need to be aware of this side of the gay scene without becoming bogged down or over-fascinated by it.

An understanding of the roots of homosexual feelings ... will help those seeking to minister to the homosexual struggler to have informed compassion.

Choice without volition?

It is often a common presumption that gay people choose to live the gay lifestyle, perhaps because we live in a permissive society where such things are more or less acceptable, or even because we think that gay people are particularly sinful and wish to push their lifestyles to the extreme. However, the reality is that homosexuality as an orientation is rarely a conscious choice. There will be many who would wish to change their feelings of same-sex attraction, and are shocked and unhappy when these feelings first become apparent. Certainly, there are people who choose to sleep with people of the same sex out of curiosity, or to exercise their sexual liberty, and a small minority claim to indulge in gay sex in order to make a political point.[5] For the majority, however, it is not a lifestyle choice.

Understanding this should make a radical difference to the way that Christians treat gay people. We will realize that expecting the gay community to repent of being homosexual (particularly in isolation from a conversion to Christianity) is fruitless. Rather, we should be seeking to lead them to repentance of *all* their sins and rejection of God, and then supporting them as they struggle on with their sexual temptations and feelings, to whatever degree, after conversion. While it is true that when we give our lives to Christ we are a new creation, we can no more expect a person's homosexual feelings to vanish at that point than we can honestly say our own sinful tendencies left us at conversion. We are all a work of sanctification in progress, in our sexuality as well as in every other area.

God has one context for sexual expression, into which homosexual conduct does not fit.

Nature or nurture?

So are people with a genuine homosexual orientation born that way, or is it something that develops in childhood? In short, is nature or nurture responsible?

It is worth noting that this, like the issue of biblical interpretation, is an issue that has been the subject of much debate among those advocating either the 'nature' or the 'nurture' aspect of the roots of homosexual orientation. Bancroft, in a *British Journal of Psychiatry* editorial,[6] wrote, 'This is an area, par excellence, where scientific objectivity has little chance of survival.' I will first look very briefly at the evidence for a biological determinism. Then I will try to give an overview of the evidence for the complex psychological roots of the orientation, before leading on to some hopeful ways forward.

Nature

Since 1993 there have been various claims in the mass media of a 'gay gene'. Although the suggestion of a biological determinism for homosexual orientation is one that still rears its head from time to time today,[7] the findings have now largely been dismissed. I will not be majoring on the science in this chapter, as there is not enough space here to go into detail about X and Y chromosomes,[8] hormonal imbalances and genetic determinism, but I will offer one example in order to make an overall point.

In 1991, a neurologist called Dr Simon Levay published an article in *Science* magazine, claiming to have found physiological differences in the brains of homosexual men and those of heterosexuals. This was sensationalized in the media and accepted uncritically by many readers, but it has subsequently been shown that Levay's research methods were unreliable, for many reasons. One is that the results came from autopsies, so there was no way of substantiating the sexual activities of the men in question. Another is that there is no evidence to suggest that the differences in the brains were causative rather than symptomatic of the sexual difference in the men. Furthermore, the sample size was just thirty-five, too small to be considered of statistical significance. The same study has since been repeated by other neuroanatomists, with stricter controls,[9] but to date Levay's findings have not been replicated.

... the reality is that homosexuality as an orientation is rarely a conscious choice.

It may seem odd that anyone would engage in, and publicize, such bad science, except if there were a definite agenda in directing public opinion in this way. In 1973, the American Psychiatric Association removed homosexuality from its list of psychiatric disorders,[10] and reclassified it as a 'condition'. The implications of this are that a homosexual would no longer have to feel that there was 'something wrong with them', but simply that they were born with a characteristic, like having blue eyes, and could accept and affirm this aspect of themselves. Saying that homosexuality is something you are born with also implies that a 'cure' for homosexuality is implausible, since to seek to cure something genetically inherited is much more problematic. Anyone claiming to seek or offer such a cure is seen as attacking the positive identity of a gay person, much as it would seem offensive for anyone to offer a black person a 'cure' for their skin pigmentation. Offering a cure introduces the implication that there is something wrong with being gay. Dr Elaine Siegel, a non-Christian psychoanalyst working with homosexual women, discovered this when her patients began to see change in their orientations:

We are all a work of sanctification in progress, in our sexuality as well as in every other area.

> Although I never interpreted homosexuality as an illness, more than half of the women became fully heterosexual. This was taken by the referral source as 'betrayal of the sisters' ... Even those women who at the end of their analyses remained homosexually inclined were viewed with suspicion by their former peers.[11]

The political reasons behind false or exaggerated claims are obvious. It is understandable that a persecuted minority would wish to promote and legitimize its existence. However, much of what the public is receiving is very difficult to substantiate. In fact, parts of the gay community itself now agree with this. An extract from an article by Peter Tatchell, a prominent and controversial gay activist, shows his incredulity over suggestions of a 'gay gene':

Much as I would love to go along with the fashionable 'born gay' consensus (it would be very politically convenient), I can't. The evidence does not support the idea that sexuality is a fixed biological given.[12]

Saying that homosexuality is something you are born with also implies that a 'cure' for homosexuality is implausible.

There are numerous other examples[13] of similar experiments, with large loopholes and conjectured conclusions. As a basis for determining a genetic or biological cause for a homosexual orientation, they can, I believe, be largely dismissed. Writing in the *Journal of Homosexuality*, McGuire concludes, 'Any genetic study must use:

1. Valid and precise measures of individual differences
2. Appropriate methods to ascertain biological relationships
3. Research subjects who have been randomly recruited
4. Appropriate sample sizes
5. Appropriate genetics models to interpret the data.

To date, all studies of the genetic basis of sexual orientation of men and women have failed to meet one or more or any of the above criteria.'[14] However, we cannot completely dismiss all the findings in this arena, as there is enough evidence to suggest *some* genetic influence on homosexual orientation. Many of the tests and experiments undertaken (though universally unreliable due to the absence of one or more of the above five points) had enough data to make a complete rejection of the possibility of genetic influence an irresponsible conclusion. For example, an experiment in 1995[15] showed that genetic implants have induced homosexual behaviour (!) in fruit flies, and a study in 1986[16] of a small sample of homosexual monozygotic (identical) twins who were reared apart, had some compelling evidence for genetic factors in the male twins. We cannot make conclus-ive statements based on animal behaviour or very small samples, but we also cannot ignore the existence of a small amount of evidence. It is fair to conclude that like many human traits, homosexual orientation is likely to be a product of more than one input. This will include genetic influences as well as environment and choice. It is important to be humble and open to new ideas and research, while also being shrewd and discerning in this area. An article[17] in *Nucleus* sums this up well:

The evidence does not support the idea that sexuality is a fixed biological given.

It certainly is easy to bring preconceptions to scientific investigation. We are always tempted to view the facts selectively in order to verify our convictions. Researchers who have the added motivation of changing public opinion will be guided along certain channels in their work. Journalists can bring their private social agendas to bear by selective and sensational reporting of research findings. Tenuous conjecture is portrayed as certain conclusion to a gullible public. Of course, it's quite appropriate for the public to be responsibly informed about scientific discoveries; however, twenty-second sound-bites cannot do justice to complex controversies.

Equally, Christians have to be careful not to fall into the same trap; we must not selectively use scientific findings to bolster our own position. The biblical injunction to 'enquire, probe and investigate it thoroughly' (Deuteronomy 13:14) is good advice. As the Bible leads us to question our interpretation of scientific facts, so new discoveries may lead us to question whether we have interpreted the Bible correctly. Revelation and science need to be balanced in the humble search for truth; properly interpreted, they should not contradict one another.

It is also important to note that, even with the possibility of genetic influence, we cannot therefore conclude that something is part of God's will. A hereditary tendency towards alcohol addiction does not mean that it was God's will for a person to become an alcoholic. Genes too are affected by the fall, and so genetic dispositions do not make us morally exempt from culpability. The possibility of genetic influence has as many implications for our pastoral response to people struggling with homosexual orientation as it would if the causes were one hundred per cent environmental – it is important to have compassion for something that is beyond a person's control, while at the same time holding them responsible for their choices in acting on their tendencies.

Genes too are affected by the fall, and so genetic dispositions do not make us morally exempt from culpability.

With all this in mind, it seems to me that there is a greater body of evidence for the psychosocial, or environmental, model of causation – that is to say that a person's upbringing and social situation can affect that person's psychological growth, having an impact on the development of their sexuality. I will spend the rest of the chapter exploring this.

Nurture

Suggesting that a homosexual orientation is environmentally caused does not necessarily imply that deliberate neglect or abuse has been present in the background of a homosexual. Often, gay people will be happy to celebrate a healthy family background, but there will still be factors, however small, that will have contributed to their sexual development. Sometimes this can be because the child has negatively misinterpreted perfectly harmless events. For example, if Dad is angry and frustrated because the car has broken down, particularly sensitive children might direct this anger onto themselves. Repeated misreadings like this may accumulate and lead to damaged self-esteem or sexuality, even though nothing remotely abusive ever took place. There are countless other situations that could lead to a similar outcome.

There is no formula that leads a person to the conclusion of a homosexual orientation.

There is no formula that leads a person to the conclusion of a homosexual orientation: for example, 'Domineering same-sex parent + rejection from peers + sexual abuse = homosexual'. The factors are far more complex and wide-ranging. While there are many key, core environmental factors that will affect the development of a person's sexuality, one person may have five of these present and another may have a different five altogether. This is why no simple formula can be applied.

There is also an element of 'nature' involved, in that things are also dependent on the disposition and sensitivity of the child in the first place, and on the reactions of the child to the environment or to events. While two siblings may have exactly the same upbringing and family situation, perhaps only one will experience struggles with their sexuality later in life, while the other is able to relate well heterosexually.[18] One child simply has a different disposition from the other, and has dealt with the same things in a different way.[19]

Same-sex parent

One of the most important studies on the roots of a homosexual orientation is *Homosexuality: A New Christian Ethic*. Its author, Elizabeth Moberly, is known as the originator of gender-affirmative therapy for homosexuality. In her study, she proposes that homosexual feelings result mainly from an 'un-met love-need' from the same-sex parent. This can be caused by an enormous spectrum of events and does not necessarily imply neglect on the part of the parent. One lesbian struggler believes that a major root of her issues lies in the fact that she had bad eczema as a tiny baby. This meant that it was physically very painful for her to be touched by her mother. Though this was not deliberate neglect on her mother's part, the child was missing out on legitimate physical affirmation from her same-sex parent.

Problems can also occur as a result of an extreme violation, such as sexual abuse, as well as from something as apparently innocuous as a word, action or attitude that is interpreted by the child as hurtful.

If something happens to break the trust between a child and the same-sex parent, the child must adopt strategies to cope with this deficit. 'Defensive detachment' is one such strategy, meaning that the child will put up an unconscious emotional 'barrier' between self and parent. This means that the child is protected from painful things being received again, but also that positive things can no longer be received. So, if a child has been touched inappropriately on one occasion, defensive detachment will mean that even healthy touching and hugs will not be received emotionally. Effectively, it will be as if the child had never been hugged or received healthy physical affirmation.

Similarly, if a child has been hurt emotionally, defensive detachment will mean that the child will be protected from further hurt, but will also be unable to receive positive emotional affirmation from the parent, because the defensive wall cannot discriminate between what is painful and what is good and healthy. Ruth's story is a good example of this:

When I was three, my sister Emily was born, but the pregnancy was really complicated. Emily was very premature and my mum was seriously ill and in hospital a lot. My earliest memory is of standing in my grandparents' hall saying 'Where's Mum?' They probably told me that she was at the hospital, but I was old enough to know that everything felt different and was not how it should be. I didn't understand why Mum wasn't there. Looking back, I think that probably did trigger a distancing between me and Mum, because I grew up with the impression that she was quite remote and very demanding of me and not very nurturing or affectionate. In reality, I don't think that's how she is, but I think I made a conscious decision at the time to withdraw from her in order to prevent myself getting hurt. I think at times I put up a wall that it was impossible for her love to get round. Even looking in my diaries from when I was a teenager, Mum was actually a lot more sympathetic and nurturing than I thought she was. However, somewhere along the line the communication channels were broken and I wasn't able to receive the nurture that she was giving. That only really started to get healed when I prayed about it.

There were things that she did wrong as well – it wasn't all me putting up defensive barriers. She wasn't terribly tactile or encouraging, but it was only through praying specifically that I would forgive her for things that there was a real transformation in our relationship.

When defensive detachment occurs, the legitimate needs of the child still remain, but the adult has no way of meeting these emotional needs any more, as the child is no longer able to respond to the adult's attempts at emotional support. These unmet needs are basic, intrinsic needs for healthy psychological growth, and will remain with the child into adulthood. An adult is long past the stage when those childhood needs can be met by the parent, but the person must meet that deficit somehow. These needs will often become sexualized during puberty, resulting in homosexual feelings. This is essentially a person trying to seek the unmet love-needs from the same-sex parent through another same-sex adult. Mark describes his own experiences:

These unmet needs are basic, intrinsic needs for healthy psychological growth, and will remain with the child into adulthood.

I was adopted and didn't find out who my real dad was until I was quite old. I'd always been searching for that. My mother is a pretty strong character and the man she married is a lovely Christian bloke, but he's mild mannered, so I didn't really have a very authoritative male figure while growing up. I was quite slow developmentally and I wasn't particularly good at sport, and I began to idolize the older boys in school – the sports heroes. As I went through puberty, that kind of became a bit sexualized and I began to look at them in more of a lustful way.

Dr Elizabeth Moberly describes the homosexual condition as 'same-sex ambivalence'. By this she means that there is both a positive and a negative (positive meaning 'towards', rather than 'good') response to the problem with the same-sex parent. Negatively, the child will disidentify with the same-gender role model. This can be observed easily in effeminate gay men or 'butch' gay women. The person has effectively said to themselves: 'If this is what a man/woman is, then I don't want to be a man/woman.'[20] In response they have subconsciously rejected attributes that represent the maleness or femaleness of the same-sex parent.

> *In response they have subconsciously rejected attributes that represent the maleness or femaleness of the same-sex parent.*

There is a spectrum in the extent to which this may happen, hence the explanation of why these stereotypes are not always present. The most extreme disidentification is transexualism: the tragic experience of a person psychologically detached from their physiological body, feeling that the only resolution is to change gender.

On the flip side of this negative reaction there is also an opposite reparative or 'positive' reaction. This is seen most clearly in the homosexual's desire for same-sex intimacy, which Moberly sees as an unconscious attempt to make up for what was not received from the same-sex parent.

Steve's father was a hard-working businessman and consequently spent little time with his family at home. Steve can remember feeling the absence of his father very keenly from an early age and this was exacerbated by a sense that his father felt ill-equipped for the job of 'Daddy' in the rare times that he was there. Steve just never really felt connected with his father. He now sees that his way of coping with this pain as a young child was to detach himself from his father, seeing the attempt at bonding as futile. He was then unable to achieve even the positive affirmations of masculinity that his dad tried to offer, and entered puberty feeling very insecure as a male. When he tried to relate to his peers, he found that he just didn't know how to do this properly – their banter felt like a foreign language that he could never quite grasp. He had never been able to learn this basic way of relating when he was a very young boy. Consequently, he has a great deficit in the development of his masculinity. He has a legitimate unmet need. This need became sexualized in puberty and he felt an overwhelming attraction towards other men. His own masculinity was so foreign to him that members of his own sex became like a fascinating 'other' that he longed to explore. Steve was desperate to fill that masculine deficit with the masculinity of others. This felt to him like strong homosexual attraction.

Steve was desperate to fill that masculine deficit with the masculinity of others.

Although this is a classic example, Steve's background is a familiar one and there will be many men who experienced a similar upbringing but never had any kind of struggle with their sexuality. As I said at the beginning of this argument, there is no formula. Other children in this situation may cope in ways other than defensive detachment, or there may have simply been something in Steve's disposition that meant that this situation led to a distortion of the development of his sexuality.

One of the most difficult things, especially from a Christian point of view, is that this raises painful questions about the parenting skills of the families of our gay friends. It's very important to stress that this is not a forum for blame. All parents are trying to bring up children in a world ravaged by sin. They themselves bear the wounds of having been raised by broken parents: a pattern that continues right back to Adam and Eve. Since no parent can ever do the job perfectly, all of us bear the wounds of having not received perfect, unconditional love. The fruits of this will manifest themselves differently in every person, but they will be present in every person, whether that person is aware of them or not. No one is completely secure about every aspect of their self or their relationships. We are all the products of the families from which we come, and since none of these environments can have been perfect in a fallen world, we all bear a spectrum of wounds and insecurities, some of which will be more significant or visible than others.

Most of us will acknowledge that our sexuality and desires are far from what God intended them to be.

Our sexuality is one vulnerable aspect of ourselves that can get damaged. Most of us will acknowledge that our sexuality and desires are far from what God intended them to be. All of us have a distorted sexuality. Some will struggle with promiscuity, some with masturbation, and some with lustful thoughts. Another such distortion is developing an attraction for members of the same sex.

All of us need God to heal these wounds. He is the only one able to offer this perfect, unconditional love. Some wounds are deeper than others, but God is willing and able to address them all: 'He heals the broken-hearted and binds up their wounds' (Psalm 147:3). In order for this to happen, we must name sin as sin, whether it has been done through ignorance or omission or by a deliberate act, and only when we recognize and name accurately the evil done to us, or in which we have participated, can we truly forgive or repent.

Jeanette Howard (author of *Out of Egypt* and *Into the Promised Land*, both written for Christians struggling with lesbianism) provides a helpful illustration of the process of sexual development:

> When you're born, it's like you are a seed planted in the soil. The soil represents the environment you're in – all those things around you that you really don't have any control over. Such as being born into an alcoholic, single-parent or abusive family. Perhaps the dad here is passive and the mum is domineering. This 'soil' environment would also cover all kinds of victimisation – things that happen to you that you don't have much control over ... As with any seed, you're going to react to your environment. You take in nutrients and poisons from the soil around you, and your seed puts out roots. And you do have control over your roots, because those are your reactions over a period of time to what's in the soil ... [for example] If a man sexually abused you as a child, that's an event you couldn't control. You were a victim. But your reaction toward that molestation helps dictate how the tree will grow. As the root grows over time, it supports a shoot that eventually becomes the tree trunk. The shoot shapes the general condition of the trunk, which then determines the kind of fruit you'll be able to grow on your tree. Ultimately, roots strongly influence your crop of fruit.[21]

This is a helpful way of describing the situation, because it shows the causative nature of sexual development, as well as showing the balance between the things we have control over and the things we do not. None of us can choose our 'soil' and no parent can give their child a perfect sin-free environment in which to begin life. However, we all react to these environments, to cope with and compensate for those imperfections. Our own personality type and, to some extent, personal responsibility, come in here. That's why, although two siblings may have exactly the same 'soil', only one may develop same-sex intimacy issues, because of their own reactions and personality type.

Opposite-sex parents

There can be so many factors that can damage the healthy sexual development of a young man or woman. The relationship with the opposite-sex parent is almost as important as that with the same-sex parent, because it is through that person that we learn about the opposite gender. If a young man has a mother who is manipulative, he may learn from that as a young child that 'all women are manipulative'. He may make an unconscious vow to avoid relating to women so that he will never be rendered powerless by their manipulation, finding it safer to relate to other men. A young girl may have a cold and distant father. She may conclude as a child that men are emotionless and impenetrable and tar all men with the same brush, affecting her adult relationships with them. She may also project this view of the father figure onto her heavenly Father, and find it very difficult to accept God's loving, tender and compassionate attributes.

> *The relationship with the opposite-sex parent is almost as important as that with the same-sex parent, because it is through that person that we learn about the opposite gender.*

Ruth recalls her relationship with her father:

I remember him shouting at me and smacking me when I did things wrong. I remember when I wouldn't wear some wellies once and he pulled me up by my wrist and was hitting me as I spun round. But most of the time he didn't get very involved in my life. I remember when I was a teenager I never knew what he thought about anything. In a way it was just like he was this strange man who lived in our house. We didn't really engage and we didn't have conversations. It was so weird when we were in the house and it was just the two of us, because we just didn't know what to say to each other, so we usually avoided each other to save embarrassment. When he took me somewhere in the car, the only way to get a conversation out of him was to ask how something worked, and then he'd explain it. He also did have quite a bad temper, and he'd hold grudges for ages. I'd do something and he'd fly off the handle about it and then he'd list all these things I'd done wrong that he'd stored up over the month. So I suppose I just thought he was a stranger who lived in our house and got angry sometimes.

We learn about relationships and ourselves from the way in which our family relates and the way in which our family views us as individuals.

This was Ruth's model for what a man – a father or a husband – was like, so her view of men, fathers and husbands in general will have been coloured by this.

Other factors

We learn about relationships and ourselves from the way in which our family relates and the way in which our family views us as individuals.

Adam recalls:

All I can really remember about my family as a kid is that Mum and Dad were always fighting. My sisters and I would always try to play outside or have really noisy games inside so that we wouldn't hear them. The worst thing was when Dad found out that Mum had been having an affair. It was just horrible and my view of Mum really changed. Dad got really paranoid and was always on about how he couldn't trust her. I kind of felt the same, really. I guess I find it hard to trust women now as an adult. I know it's sort of irrational, because not every woman is like my mum! But I guess I'm just still a bit affected by all that. It was a pretty big deal.

Relationships with other significant people will also have an impact on our development and sense of self. Siblings, aunts, uncles, teachers and other key adults all have an important role as they interact with the child.

Another factor that can affect the development of our sexuality is our relationships with our peers. When we enter the school playground, we enter as the product of our lives so far: the product of an imperfect family with an imperfect self-image. Each of these incomplete, insecure people is trying to survive and compete, often at the expense of one another's feelings. According to an NSPCC report in 2000,[22] 43% of young people had experienced either physical bullying, discrimination, or being made to feel different by other children. The report said:

When we enter the school playground, we enter as the product of our lives so far: the product of an imperfect family with an imperfect self-image.

Although relatively little of the bullying took a physical form, this in no way means that it was less serious or harmful for the children on the receiving end, particularly if the non-physical forms constituted a prolonged attack on the child's self-esteem and self-confidence. It is notable that most of the issues about which respondents said they were bullied – their size, intelligence, social background and race – were fundamental aspects of their identity over which they had no control, so that bullying would represent a major psychological attack.

School, and acceptance or otherwise by our peers, is a crucial time for the forming of a child's sense of identity. A child's place in the pecking order at school, or a name given cruelly, can stay long into adult years. Joshua tells of his school experiences:

> I was always one of the kids who were always the last to be picked for sport. I was bullied at school and I had a really low self-esteem. I just thought everybody disliked me. I had a few friends, but they were the sort of kids that I guess grouped together – the sad cases in the choir! And so, being bullied I guess made my self-esteem pretty low. There was a whole class at primary school that used to call me Nancy. I don't know whether that had a huge effect on me, but it certainly made me feel inadequate, and that was horrible.

School, and acceptance or otherwise by our peers, is a crucial time for the forming of a child's sense of identity.

In this case, Joshua's school experiences are unlikely to be the primary root of his sexuality struggles, but they will have been a significant addition to his already damaged self-image. The unmet childhood need for positive affirmation was escalated, and so too was his desire to get those needs met homosexually.

Individual traumatic events can also have a very significant effect on the development of a person's sexuality. Although the existence of sexual abuse or incest (whether heterosexual or homosexual in nature) is not a guarantee of future homosexual orientation, nor do gay feelings imply a history of the same, there is a fairly high correlation between the two.

Healing

Once the homosexual desire is understood in these terms, it becomes clear that what is needed for the homosexual struggler is much compassion and grace. The gay person should not be surprised that the need for a partner can feel so overwhelming and painful. This need is not just about sex or companionship; it's about very basic human needs being unmet for a long time. It is true that the apparent reparative solution of a same-sex lover is not the answer, but understanding this does not remove the unmet need. Andrew Comiskey (author of *Pursuing Sexual Wholeness: How Jesus Heals the Homosexual* and founder of the Living Waters programme[23] puts it like this:

They will need friends who can love them, remind them of the gospel and lead them back to Christ with patience, as often as that is needed.

The homosexual tendencies [the individual] faces are really red flag warnings that deeper, non-erotic needs are surfacing from the soul.

When strugglers understand there's a normal and legitimate need at the core of their sexual tendencies, they find the truth liberating. They aren't perverts who love evil for evil's sake. An innocent, involuntary need is expressing itself in a broken way.

That grants them the profound freedom to care for their needs while not submitting them to a false solution.[24]

The friend wishing to minister to the homosexual should not be surprised, either, if their friend just 'keeps messing up'. So much grace is needed. Sin should never be excused, but much compassion is needed for the extent of the battle on the hands of the homosexual struggler. They will need friends who can love them, remind them of the gospel and lead them back to Christ with patience, as often as that is needed.

It's important to note, then, that sexual abstinence, although absolutely right and necessary, is not a solution to the issue. The homosexual is still left with these glaring unmet needs. The possibility of healing becomes desirable. Healing does not necessarily imply the happy-ever-after of spouse and kids, but rather a moving towards healthier same-sex and opposite-sex relating. There is a spectrum for what healing might look like. Since the issue is more complex than a preference for members of the same sex, the solution is not, as many often think, finding someone of the opposite sex.

One key solution lies in healthy non-sexual, non-emotionally dependent same-sex friendships.

I am constantly being re-assured by loving friends that soon I shall meet a guy whom I really like and get married, and that everything will be OK! These friends are only trying to be kind, but this is sometimes painful to hear, simply because I would love it to be true. The fact is, however, that I know that things are much more complex and deep rooted. Marriage is not the solution to the problem, since the deficit is a problem with same-sex relating. Improved opposite-sex relating will not address the same-sex issue in any way. One key solution, therefore, lies in *healthy* non-sexual, non-emotionally dependent same-sex friendships. Attaining this will involve healing at the root.

Jeanette Howard's tree analogy is again helpful here. We all begin as seeds planted in soil. We have no control over the soil we are in, which is the environment we are born into. We may be a wanted child in a loving, stable family. Or we may be an unplanned child in a dysfunctional, violent situation. Or we may well be anywhere on the spectrum in between. Our roots are our reactions to our soil. We may react bitterly or angrily, or by shutting down. We may also have healthy responses to good things. The roots take this stuff up the trunk of the plant. The kind of fruit that we produce will be fed by the nutrients or poisons carried by our roots. The analogy continues as we see that we cannot simply pluck off the fruit to remove our sinful behaviour resulting from our background. We must deal with it at the root if we are to produce good fruit.

We should not be surprised if the homosexual condition cannot be healed with one prayer and the laying-on of hands.

Our response

Understanding all this helps us in our approach to seeking any kind of healing or degree of change in orientation. We should not be surprised if the homosexual condition cannot be healed with one prayer and the laying-on of hands. On one level, we are asking a psychological child to grow up to the age of the physiological adult. We cannot expect this to happen overnight! We *must* pray, and we can absolutely trust that prayer can and does heal in this way, but patience is also needed because of the nature of the issue being addressed. God needs to be invited into every aspect of our wounded histories, and this can be a long and painful process. Homosexual healing ministries can be a useful tool in this, as each stage of development can be addressed in a safe and informed environment.[25]

Mike Haley[26] makes the following comments when discussing the process of leaving homosexuality behind:

> Make no mistake about it – leaving homosexuality is not easy. Many gay men and women do start the healing process, only to drop out when the going gets tough.[27]

He offers this hope:

> So is there hope for change? Yes, but whether a homosexual desiring change seeks his or her answer in the reality of unbiased psychological study ... or in the undeniable truth of the Bible found in 1 Corinthians ['and that is what some of you *were*', 1 Corinthians 6:11], that person must be highly motivated and 'hold unswervingly to the hope [we] profess, for he who promised is faithful' (Hebrews 10:23).[28]

God knows exactly where we are and he will provide all that we need to fight whatever battles we must contend with at any particular time.

While discussing healing, it is important to note that God does not promise to heal us completely while we are on earth. It is true that God promises to finish the work that he began in us,[29] and this should spur us on in hope – we *are* being sanctified daily to become more and more like Christ, if we are actively seeking to co-operate with the ministry of the Holy Spirit in us, and this absolutely includes the area of our sexuality. However, we must hold this in tension with the fact that there are many who have prayed for years and still struggle a great deal; and I am one of those. This may mean 'not yet' or it may mean 'not till glory', but we can be sure that God will not abandon us. He knows exactly where we are and he will provide all that we need to fight whatever battles we must contend with at any particular time.

It's also important not to make our definition of 'healing' too narrow. It does not only have to mean a complete change from homosexuality to heterosexuality. Although I personally feel that my attraction to other women has not diminished much since becoming a Christian, I *can* see a great deal of change in my healthy relating to people of the opposite sex. Whereas, before conversion, I could not have counted a single male friend, I can now say that I enjoy many healthy friendships with guys. This is definitely because of God's intervention and is a great testimony to his sanctifying work in me. It makes sense that he would not want me to ignore fifty per cent of the population, even if marriage is never part of his plan for me! It's helpful sometimes to start with smaller goals towards wholeness, and to acknowledge and praise God in them as change occurs.

It's helpful sometimes to start with smaller goals towards wholeness, and to acknowledge and praise God in them as change occurs.

I believe that the most helpful attitude for a friend of a homosexual struggler to have is one of acceptance. It is right to offer hope of healing and to pray actively and patiently for that. It is also right not to demand results from God in this. It is right not to make assumptions about God, or to lay these assumptions on the struggler, giving them false reassurances of future marriage and family. It is absolutely right and best to love, support and accept the friend in the stage that they have reached, and to walk beside them in the hopes, disappointments, joys and progress that will follow.

4

Identity and evangelism

Ella says:

> It *is* scary to think of having to witness to gay people.
> Partly because it's a scary environment in that the gay
> scene, if you're not gay, can be quite intimidating. But the
> main reason is because you're just always dreading that
> question: 'What do you think about homosexuality?' It's
> hard to know how honest to be and whether just to skirt
> around the issue, or whether to tell them what the Bible
> really says. That's quite a hard thing to do because you're
> afraid of how they might react.[1]

Why do we sometimes find gay people so difficult to witness
to? Why does the gospel seem so much more offensive to them
than it does to our straight friends? Why are gay people sometimes
so aggressively anti-Christian?

It is important for Christians to find the answers to these
questions, so that we can witness compassionately and effectively.
In order to grasp this, we need a better understanding of the issue

of *identity* for a gay person, and also to take a look at how Christians seem from a gay point of view. It is often hard to see ourselves as we appear to others.

Identity

Sometimes it is hard for heterosexuals to see just how much gay people feel that their sexuality is intrinsic to their identity. All of us define our individual identity according to groups that we feel that we belong to:

> *All of us define our individual identity according to groups that we feel that we belong to.*

Instead of simply being a person with particular characteristics, we can begin to think of ourselves in terms of our group memberships and say about ourselves, for instance, 'I am a Catholic'; 'I am a British citizen'; 'I am a single parent'; 'I am an OU student'; 'I am a member of the Labour Party'. As we label ourselves in this way (or are labelled by others) our sense of who we are and what we are like changes.[2]

For a heterosexual, sexual preference is an almost incidental thing. It is a 'normal' and natural part of life, whether one chooses to express it or not. Heterosexuals are unlikely to consider their heterosexuality as something that marks them out as belonging to a particular group (a heterosexual subculture), so as such it does not influence the forming of individual identity in the way described above. It is just the norm.

Minority groups

It is not shocking or unsettling to find oneself attracted to the opposite sex. There is no sense of a need to seek out others who feel the same way and understand. (We live in such a sex-saturated society that it is almost impossible *not* to find others who feel the same way and understand!)

It is only when we are part of a minority group that we feel the need to identify ourselves strongly with that group. The smaller the minority and the more that minority is attacked by the majority, the more strongly this need for identification is felt.

For example, it is only when I am in a foreign country that I bother to feel particularly English. The rest of the time I am surrounded by other English people and I don't give it a second thought. It is the thing that makes me different from those around me that I am most acutely conscious of. When I am the only English person in the room, I want to assert and affirm all that makes me English. If someone asks me the question 'Who are you?' I am far more likely to answer 'I am English' near the beginning of my description of myself than I would be in a room full of English people. If the other people in the room were speaking negatively about English people, I would feel an even stronger need to assert my positive position as an English person.

It is the thing that makes me different from those around me that I am most acutely conscious of.

Brian, a non-Christian, experienced this need to assert his sexual identity.

I remember a time when I'd just started in a new job. I was in the tea room for my break and there was all this homophobic banter going on. It made me feel so awkward and small and excluded. My reaction was to feel angry because I felt the things they were saying were so unreasonable. They didn't know anything about me, and yet they were ridiculing me without even knowing.

I was angry because they were saying things like this about my friends that were gay too. All the people in my life that were important to me were being humiliated by these people.

I'm not the kind of person to sit back in silence in a situation like that; I'm not just going to lie down and take it. I confronted them with my sexuality, and I guess I camped it up a bit more than maybe I would have otherwise. I wanted to be *so gay*, so that they knew that this was who I was and that I was proud of it, and that they were wrong to say the things they said. It felt good to be out and proud and strong. It helped me not to feel like I did when I first went in there and I was this unknown, and I'd felt so ashamed and weak.

> *Gay people often feel an acute sense of 'differentness'.*

Perhaps this has a lot to do with why gay people often feel that their sexuality is one of the most important aspects of who they are. Gay people often feel an acute sense of 'differentness'. Many social psychologists say that the more we feel that an aspect of who we are is in the minority, or that our group is weak or under attack, the more our sense of identity and self-esteem feels threatened, so the stronger the need to assert and affirm this aspect of ourselves.[3]

The group to which a person belongs serves as a primary determinant of his self-esteem. To a considerable extent, personal feelings of worth depend on the social evaluation of the group with which a person is identified. Self-hatred and feelings of worthlessness tend to arise from membership in underprivileged or outcast groups.[4]

An unsettling discovery

When gay people first begin to realize that they are feeling attraction towards members of their own sex, there are a few ways to respond. Few people are initially pleased when they realize that they are experiencing gay feelings. Few people feel that they want to share it straight away. Generally, people do not naturally think of homosexuality as desirable, or the gay community as a strong group that they would want to be a part of, even in a liberal, pluralistic and politically correct society. Most heterosexual people do not wish that they were gay. I think this has a lot to do with how the homosexual group is viewed by society. On finding themselves to have a homosexual orientation, most people are more likely to find it quite an unsettling discovery initially, regardless of whether or not they embrace it later in life.

Laura describes how she felt when she first began to realize she was attracted to members of the same sex.

> Firstly I think I was surprised and kind of shocked. And I just really felt ashamed. A huge sense of shame, but you know, at the same time it was exciting in a way. But I wouldn't allow myself to think too hard on it.

And Rosie:

> Well, I think that when I first thought about it – when I had some first thoughts – I put them to the back of my mind for a lot of years, and I told everybody that I thought people being gay disgusted me.

All this goes a long way towards explaining the aggressive 'in your face-ness' of parts of the gay community and, more importantly, why Christians are often met with such defensive reactions when they try to share the gospel with gay people. No one enjoys feeling bad about oneself, so naturally one will make adjustments:

Feeling good about oneself, evaluating oneself positively, feeling that one is a person of worth, have been described as a basic goal of the self-concept, a basic human need ... According to self-esteem maintenance assumptions, all else being equal, individuals prefer to feel good about themselves and so will self-define in such a way as to maintain positive self-feelings.[5]

So the group that we belong to must be defended and promoted in order to preserve a positive self-esteem. Homophobia is a direct attack on this, and the Christian gospel is perceived by many as homophobic and thus an attack on a gay person's core identity and sense of value.

The usual story

Now put all of this in the context of a gay person's likely personal history. Puberty is a difficult time for anybody, straight or gay: we are trying to work out who we are, our bodies are changing and our hormones are making us feel new and strange things. Because a lot of these changes have to do with our sexuality, most of them are private adjustments, and although most of us know that what we are going through is a normal part of life and our bodies are changing in a perfectly natural way, it is still often an embarrassing and strange experience.

For a schoolboy who finds himself attracted to other boys, this whole experience is made far more confusing. Put yourself in Simon's shoes.

As Simon's friends are becoming more and more interested in their female classmates, Simon finds that he is experiencing these same feelings towards one or two of his male mates and still has no interest in girls. He knows that this makes him different, and to feel different at this age is horrible. He wants to be like his friends and to be able to join in with their conversations and feelings. He does not understand why he feels this way about some of his friends and he feels ashamed and disgusted with himself initially. It's not normal; he is not like his other friends. He is afraid of what people might think if they knew, and he hopes that it is a phase that will go away.

After a while, he plucks up the courage to tell a few trusted friends, and he finds that he is accepted. However, it is not long before he discovers that there are some who have strong negative feelings towards those who feel the way that he does. In fact, he is already well aware of aspects of this. He knows that 'gay' and 'lesbian' are used as derogatory names at his school. He knows that, even in a world of increasing political correctness, to be gay is considered, at least by his school peers, as something worthy of derision and ridicule. He is acutely aware of this, and feels alone and isolated because he does not know of anyone else who feels the same way.

As it becomes clear that Simon's feelings are not part of a passing phase, he decides to learn to accept the way that he feels. One way that he does this is to seek out others who feel the same way. As he begins to visit gay bars and to seek out other gay

> *He feels alone and isolated because he does not know of anyone else who feels the same way.*

people, he begins to experience some of the things that he so painfully missed out on as he was growing up. He finds that here he is no longer 'different'; he fits in, he has a place where he belongs. For the first time he feels free to be himself, to be honest and real without fear of rejection, because he knows that the people here mirror how he feels. He can *accept* himself here. He feels as if he has come home after a long time of being a foreigner.

However, as soon as he steps outside this bubble he is more acutely aware than before of the difference between people within it and those outside, and of the hostility that people feel towards the group. Outsiders are the majority and so they seem to him to act with arrogance. He becomes aware that gay people have fewer civil rights; that their preferences and needs are not catered for or represented as much. In some places he cannot be free to be honest about 'who he really is' without fear of persecution. He does not even feel free to do something as innocent as hold his boyfriend's hand in public without people staring and making comments. It seems so unfair that straight people enjoy this luxury without giving it a second thought. Whenever he opens a newspaper he sees some story of the church being homophobic and excluding gay people. It seems to him that Christians are not the loving, non-judgmental people they claim to be. They seem the worst bigots of all. He reads the history of what gay people had to suffer in the past and feels a stronger and stronger need to defend his position in the light of all the injustice.

> *... being on the receiving end of persecution and injustice will inevitably create a level of defensiveness.*

Defending the group

Simon's story helps us in a number of ways: by illustrating the reasons for such a strong sense of group identity in the gay community, and in turn why this would make evangelism more difficult for Christians. As Simon's story illustrates, being on the receiving end of persecution and injustice will inevitably create a level of defensiveness. The gay community is a minority group with a history of persecution, giving it a sense that it needs to defend itself and justify its position. Simon becomes increasingly aware of this as he begins to explore the gay community. A secular book on homosexuality concludes a chapter on historic homophobia in this way:

> The history of homophobia reveals an extraordinary array of ills laid at the door of people who depart from the heterosexual norm. They have been seen as sinful, pestilent, criminal, unnatural, sick, degenerate and unpatriotic. They have brought plague, poison, and threatened the family, state, natural order and survival of the human race. The anti-gay backlash caused by the AIDS epidemic was part of a long tradition.[6]

Mark's experience of going to gay bars shows how this alienation can be relieved by a welcoming group.

This sense of group belonging is accentuated by a sense of 'uniform' in dress, interest or mannerism.

I always found the atmosphere in gay pubs and clubs pretty friendly, and I think it's because it's full of a lot of people who feel that they don't fit in society, so they really make an effort to fit with one another. You tend to find that you've got a lot in common because you've probably suffered from discrimination or perhaps estrangement from your family or some pretty serious life issues, and yet you can get together and have a good time and I just found it fun and non-threatening.

This sense of group belonging is accentuated by a sense of 'uniform' in dress, interest or mannerism, all contributing strongly to the sense of identity that a person will feel in being part of the gay community. This is a normal way for a group to strengthen itself: by differentiating itself from outsiders.

> The core idea is that we categorize ourselves just as we categorize others, and thus we depersonalize ourselves ... our behaviour assimilates or conforms to the relevant in-group prototype in terms of attitudes, feelings and actions.[7]

The way in which this works in the gay community is illustrated by the experiences of Mark and Clare respectively.

> I suppose there is an effect if you hang out with a lot of gay people for a long time. I probably am a little bit more effeminate in some ways. I don't think I am an effeminate person; I mean I'm quite sporty, I'm well built, I don't mince around, things like that, but I do know that if I spend time in the company of camp people I can affect a bit of the voice and I can be a bit like that myself.

> I think that in response to trying to fit in on the gay scene I've adopted more gay-type clothes and probably mannerisms.

A non-Christian called Caroline described her experience of the lesbian scene in a similar way:

> People perform their identities and in so doing they more often than not conform to a certain look. Not all people, but I admit I have been swayed to a certain degree, to be visible. People get an idea of what lesbians look like and how they behave, and if you want to be visible, to some degree you have to conform to that way of behaving and of looking to get the type of visibility that you desire. I think it's a lot to do with association; people feeling comfortable with like people, who are similar, who act

similarly. It's just a natural tendency, to be with people you're similar to and feel comfortable with. But maybe for some people in areas where [homosexuality] is very oppressed and isn't something that would go down too well, there is more of a tribe mentality: you want to really stick together for protection rather than for social reasons. But yeah, definitely, I think there is some sort of mentality amongst lesbians: 'Yeah, we're the same; let's all stick together.'

These things can be conscious or not (and are present in a different form in the Christian subculture too!), but all contribute to forming a sense of belonging and identity. It is all of these things that are felt by gay people to be attacked when Christians confront them with any suggestion that the way that they choose to express their sexuality is wrong. Not only sexual practice is being challenged.

It's just a natural tendency, to be with people you're similar to and feel comfortable with.

How does it feel?
It is really important to grasp all these things as we consider the way that we witness to our gay friends. When talking about the cost of following Jesus, while emphasizing that it is grace that saves us, we must be honest that sexual abstinence is the only biblical option for a gay person who comes to Christ. But this is *not* the same as telling our straight non-Christian friends that they should stop sleeping with their boyfriends or girlfriends.

Your straight friends will find that hard to hear and will find it difficult and painful to stop, but that is as far as it goes. They will not have to stop going to bars frequented by those who sleep with their boyfriends or girlfriends. They will not have to cut themselves off from their other straight friends. They will not have to face the likely reality that they will never have another boyfriend or girlfriend for the rest of their lives. They will not have to question their whole identity as 'a heterosexual person' and rethink all that they are and what is important to them. Gay people may have to consider any or all of these things as they weigh up the cost of following Christ.

. . . we must be honest that sexual abstinence is the only biblical option for a gay person who comes to Christ.

I would like to help the Christian reader to get into the shoes of a gay person who hears a Christian say something like: 'I really love you, but I think what you do is wrong. I think it would be better if you stopped practising your homosexuality.' I think it is helpful to imagine someone saying a similar thing to you about your Christian faith. Imagine if a person were to say to you: 'I really love you, but I just think the whole Jesus thing is wrong. I would prefer it if you stopped being a Christian'.[8] Would you not feel that you were being attacked as a *person*? What you believe is intrinsic to your identity. It informs your morality, your use of money and time, your lifestyle, your eternal destiny! For you to still be *you*, it would be impossible to take your Christian faith out of the equation.

Challenging identity

A friend of mine, Karen, has been trying to witness to Louise, a gay friend of hers. One of the things that Karen found difficult about this was that she knew that Louise was wrong about her perception of her identity. From a Christian point of view, she knew that it was wrong to define someone by their sexual preference. We are so much more than that. We are made in the image of God, so this is the answer to the question 'Who am I?' Our identity is found in this non-transient fact. We are fearfully and wonderfully made, with a purpose other than expressing a sexual preference.

Louise, however, did not acknowledge (or perhaps even know) that she was made in the image of God. For Louise, as for any non-Christian, there is no external reference (God), so her identity has to be self-referential. Non-Christians are forced, therefore, to define themselves by what they feel, what they do, what they want to do, whom they know, how much they are loved or revered, how they look, how much they earn, etc. All of these are false and weak constructs of identity, because they are all so fragile and changeable.

We are fearfully and wonderfully made, with a purpose other than expressing a sexual preference.

Without the eternal, immoveable, external reference of God, our sense of who we are is as transient and unreliable as the thing that we choose to define us. What happens if we lose our job, our status, our looks, our friends? Our self-esteem plummets because we no longer know who we are. Louise defined herself by her sexuality. So when Karen said that this was invalid, in the sense that her *true* immoveable identity was in the unchanging fact that she is made in God's image, all Louise heard was that her fundamental sense of who she is was being undermined.

The fact remains that Karen is speaking truth and reality, whereas Louise is constructing and believing something false for herself. But Karen must understand that for Louise to see this, she must have her eyes opened by the Holy Spirit. In short, she needs to become a Christian. Karen must be patient and understanding of Louise as she fails to see the truth, since 'the god of this age has blinded the minds of unbelievers, so that they cannot see the light of the gospel of the glory of Christ, who is the image of God' (2 Corinthians 4:4). Without the interaction of the Holy Spirit, none of us can naturally know the truth about God. All the intellectual understanding in the world will get us no further, unless God reveals himself as God to us. This revelation includes the knowledge of our identity as a person made in God's image. This is a spiritual truth, which cannot be gained through learning alone.

Without the interaction of the Holy Spirit, none of us can naturally know the truth about God.

So how can we reach them?

So, having acknowledged how hard and complex it all is, what on earth are we to do when we try to communicate the gospel into all of this?

The first response is not to be put off. We probably need to witness to gay people slightly differently and perhaps more sensitively than we do to some other friends, but this does not mean that we should shy away from it completely, or that it is impossible. The gay community *needs the gospel*! Our gay friends need saving from a lost eternity. We cannot let fear or ignorance stop us from fulfilling the great commission with this particular lost and neglected mission field.

It is important to be mindful of the fact that a lot of gay people will be starting with an awful lot of negative prejudice. The media are constantly presenting Christians as homophobic and unloving towards gay people. There is also the sad fact that a large proportion of Christians *are* at best misinformed, and at worst strongly homophobic,[9] so there will be a great many gay people who have first-hand negative experience of Christians. Often the best place to start is to say 'Sorry'. 'Sorry' on behalf of any Christian who has said hurtful and insensitive things and claimed that it is the Christian line, and to communicate that our own desire is to love and understand our gay friends in the best way possible, through listening and compassion.

Caroline, a non-Christian lesbian, told me about one particular experience she had had of Christian homophobia:

> When they showed the first civil partnership on TV,
> I thought, 'These two girls, it's their big day,' and it was
> really sad that there was a far-right Christian standing with
> a placard saying 'You'll rot in
> Hell'. I thought, 'Each to
> their own; you might have
> those beliefs, but why stand
> there and try and inflict
> them on someone else?'   *. . . so there will be a great*
> They're having what is, to   *many gay people who*
> them, a very important and   *have first-hand negative*
> special day. You wouldn't   *experience of Christians.*
> dream of standing up at a
> heterosexual couple's
> wedding and doing the same
> thing. I thought that was
> quite sad, actually, and reflects poorly on the Christian
> community, and I hope that's not representative of
> Christians in general.

We must be mindful of the fact that sad situations like this do exist. We need to take it into account and be sensitive in view of it when witnessing to our gay friends.

Because of this, and the generally sensitive nature of the issue, I am not convinced of the usefulness of addressing gay people en masse evangelistically: for example, distributing flyers in gay bars, or giving evangelistic talks aimed at the gay community. This is not to say that we should not be inviting our gay friends to general evangelistic events (I myself was converted by a series of general evangelistic talks), but I am very wary of evangelistic talks intentionally addressing the homosexuality issue. We need to invite our gay friends to events ourselves, so that they are going with a person who loves them. Going to a gay event uninvited, with flyers listing the relevant Bible passages, is insensitive. I think that the gospel is such an offence to gay people, and such a huge lifestyle and identity challenge, that it needs to come from a known, loving source in order to get past the possible prejudice or previous negative experience of Christianity.

When my friend first told me the gospel, I was *so* offended that she would dare to suggest that if I were to become a Christian my sexual preference would be less valid than someone else's. I think the only reason I even listened to her was that I knew she had already been a good and supportive friend for two years. I knew that she loved me and she was prepared to be my friend, knowing that I was gay. She at no point communicated that her love was conditional on my conversion (or that choosing celibacy was the condition on which I could become a Christian). She just said, very plainly, that I needed Jesus, just like everybody else, and talked about some of the implications for me. It did test our friendship, but we survived it because she had already proved that she would be saying this only out of love, not out of some misguided bigotry. In fact, her solid (though, of course, imperfect) friendship made me ask myself whether there might even be some truth in what she was saying to me. It was that which started me on the path towards accepting Christ.

> *She just said, very plainly, that I needed Jesus, just like everybody else.*

In the case of Karen and Louise, Karen felt as though she had come up against a brick wall, because Louise had been so offended by the notion that there could be anything wrong with being gay. Louise explained that she felt as though her entire identity had been attacked and she questioned Karen's love for her. In this case, it was not good enough to say 'Love the sinner, hate the sin', because Louise felt so strongly that the 'sin' was Louise herself. Her sexuality permeated every aspect of her life. If Karen was saying that Louise had to be celibate, Louise felt that Karen's love was conditional. She felt that Karen did not really love her, but that she loved a version of her that she wanted her to be, not who she really was right now.

I had to ask Karen whether there was actually any truth in what Louise was saying. Was it in fact true that Karen loved only the 'ideal' Louise, with her sexuality removed? If this really *was* the case, then there was something wrong. When we witness to our straight non-Christian friends, do we honestly feel that we will *really* be their friends only once they are 'saved and sorted'? I hope not! I hope that they are our friends and we would love them even if they were never saved, though it breaks our hearts to think of it. There is a delicate balance here. God loves us as we are; it was while we were still sinners that Christ died for the ungodly. Yet his love always tells us the truth and will not leave us as we are, no matter how hard it is to change. He loves us too for what we will be, when he has finished working on us and we are perfect in Christ, totally conformed to the image of Jesus. That is our ultimate destiny and our completed identity.

When we witness to our straight non-Christian friends, do we honestly feel that we will really be their friends only once they are 'saved and sorted'?

I am sure that we can confidently say 'Jesus loves you' to our unsaved friends, as truthfully as we can say it to our Christian brothers and sisters. We would not say 'Jesus will love you when you are saved' or 'Jesus loves most of you, but not the sinful bits'. Put like this, it is clear that Karen should love Louise as she is, but Karen had to admit that she needed to think hard about the truth of that. Perhaps the perception that homosexuality is a greater sin is so ingrained in us that we find it very hard to view it in the same way as all the other sins listed in Romans 1. If this is the case, we have to admit that our thinking has been influenced by our own prejudice or society's views, rather than by the truth that 'all have sinned and fall short of the glory of God' (Romans 3:23).

We must be able to communicate truthfully with our friends that we love them, and that there are no caveats. The fact is that a person will become a Christian only if they encounter Jesus Christ, and if they are to do that through us, then we must try to love them as he loves. This is of course true for any of our friends, but I think it is particularly important for those who are gay, because such a difficult thing can be heard only in the safety of a loving context.

Karen also found that she really needed to remind herself that the truth of the gospel really is the answer for Louise, and that it really is true and *always* true.

Karen said:

Louise presents her case so forcefully, it's really easy to wonder if I am homophobic after all ... but the truth is the gospel *is* the right perspective! It *isn't* right to define your identity in terms of your sexuality and, more specifically, it isn't right or healthy or beneficial or OK to live your life in rejection of God, because he is *good* and *right* and *in charge*.

Karen is right! It is so important that we are convinced of this ourselves before we think about challenging someone else on it, knowing that it has such huge implications for them. It can be easy to feel these convictions being undermined in the face of the strength of the gay defence. When I spoke to a non-Christian gay person this week, she gave me such a positive view of lesbian identity and lifestyle that I really found myself wondering if I was a fool! Why was I busy denying myself all this, and facing this struggle, when she is so happy and positive?

The answer is that the gospel is true, our identity in Christ is reality, and that these truths are eternal.

> But the day of the Lord will come like a thief. The heavens will disappear with a roar; the elements will be destroyed by fire, and the earth and everything in it will be laid bare.
>
> Since everything will be destroyed in this way, what kind of people ought you to be? You ought to live holy and godly lives as you look forward to the day of God and speed its coming.
> (2 Peter 3:10–12)

This life is not all there is, and the bottom line, whatever the obstacles, is that everyone needs to know and live by this truth.

We must not be discouraged by the obstacles to a gay person's becoming a Christian. We serve a God who can move mountains ('For nothing is impossible with God', Luke 1:37). To him, it is as easy to save your gay friend as it is to save the kind old lady, the terrorist, the gang member, or the five-year-old child. Keep praying, and keep loving your friend well. The rest is up to God, and he is more than able.

After conversion

> *Mark says:*
>
> I didn't realize how long it would take [to work through my sexuality issues] and how difficult it would be. But we're talking about eternity here, and there was obviously going to be a battle for my mind and for my soul. The devil has had me in this lifestyle for all those years and messing things up nicely, and does not want me to be free of it. And he really does not want me to be getting other people free of it. So I should really have foreseen a lot more of the adversity. It has been six years of very hard work, and there have been plenty of times when I've thought, 'Oh, forget this! Let's just go back to what I know,' and there was a short period when I did do that . . . but yeah, I didn't realize how difficult it was going to be.[1]

I meet a surprising number of people who honestly think that once gay people have been converted, they are no longer gay. It is true that we are a new creation when we are born again, as these people say, but sadly this does not mean an instant end to sin. This is as true for sexual struggles as it is for any others. It is easy to underestimate the amount of support that people struggling with homosexuality need when they become Christians.

Singleness

Ruth says:

I suppose I sometimes get quite afraid of the future. I'm not worried about my future after death, because I'm really looking forward to going to heaven! However, I do sometimes stress myself out with thinking too far ahead in this life. I often worry about still being all on my own when I'm eighty and being really lonely, with no one to look after me. I just try to tell myself that I will have to tackle that if and when I get to it. Being single today is mostly all right, so there's no reason to think that tomorrow is not going to be all right too.[2]

. . . lifelong singleness is a reality that many will have to face.

One of the biggest long-term issues that converted gay people need support in is their singleness. It is of course true that God can and does lead some to heterosexuality and marriage, but, for someone who has lived thus far as a homosexual and is new to the possibilities of a miraculous and healing God, this can seem like a distant and unlikely dream. Indeed, for the majority marriage is not the outcome, so lifelong singleness is a reality that many will have to face.

Singleness is a very real challenge for the church. Obviously it is an issue that goes far beyond the realm of homosexual strugglers and those ministering to them. It is a large issue for the never-married, the widowed and the divorced, to name but a few. However, we as a church have such a long way to go in this area that it is helpful to address it here. It is such a key area that it is crucial to offer long-term support for our Christian friends who are struggling with their sexuality, if the church is to live out the ideal of being members of God's family. This means finding ways of including single people in traditional family life. It means incorporating single people as equally valued members of the church, and it means putting forward the positive theology of singleness so clearly expressed in the Bible.

As I said in the first chapter, adjusting to a probable single future was one of the hardest challenges of my life. It is difficult to imagine what this can be like; there are few situations where someone will be asked to make a lifelong commitment to sexual abstinence, when celibacy is not necessarily something that he or she feels specifically called to.

> *. . . it means putting forward the positive theology of singleness so clearly expressed in the Bible.*

Personally, I had to go through a very real and painful grieving process to let go of the things that I had been living for and the dreams that I had for my future. I had to face a future of unwanted solitude, and I did not really know any more why I was alive, if it was not to love and be loved in that way.

At my conversion, like most new Christians, I had only a very basic grasp of what the gospel and the Christian life meant. I had understood that God was real, that I was a sinner and that the only thing that could save me was trusting in the death and resurrection of Jesus Christ to pay for my sin. That was all I needed to be saved, but it was an impoverished view of what God was offering me. As far as I understood, Jesus had given me a 'Get Out of Hell Free' card, so what I had to do was grin and bear a lonely life until death brought me heaven.

We must remember not to assume too much knowledge in a new convert! The only world-view I had ever been exposed to was the one presented by magazines, movies and song lyrics, which was that boy meets girl (or girl meets girl or boy meets boy!) and they live happily ever after. This is a dream that many of us have, but it is sometimes hard to accept that it may not be the reality for all of us. This is a thought pattern that is ingrained in us from a young age. Otherwise it would not be the subject of so many songs, movies and books. Most people have to spend a season of their lives as singles, and some spend the whole of their lives in this way, whether by choice or not. It is a different matter entirely to *know* that this is your lot, especially if you are converted at a young age. Much support is needed for people wrestling with this.

Team effort

The Bible is very positive about both singleness and the possibility of living a rich and fulfilling life as an unmarried person. For this to happen in reality, however, a team effort is needed. God said, right from the start, 'It is not good for man to be alone' (Genesis 2:18), so a person who is to remain unmarried will need other people around them and strong relationships and friendships outside a marriage partnership. It is those who are friends and supporters of the single person who need to rise to this challenge.

Married friends

Those who are married or have children have a great opportunity to incorporate others into their natural family life. It is not true that in the church there are those who are in families and there are those who are single. We are all one family, because we are all one body in Christ and the gospel is lived out when we live that way.

For those who follow Jesus, the critical blood, the blood that most significantly determines their identity and character, is not the blood of the biological family. It is the blood of the lamb.[3]

It takes quite a radical and countercultural mindset to think in this way – to open up your natural, physical family to include others – but Christians by their very nature are radical and countercultural people! We have the opportunity to set an example to the world, that a family does not have to be an autonomous unit, but can be completely inclusive. Single people can be additional aunts, uncles, big brothers or sisters. It is a solution for the families and for the singles. Everybody wins! Ella and Jane have enjoyed the benefits of families who have tried to live in this way:

We are all one family, because we are all one body in Christ and the gospel is lived out when we live that way.

Ella:

Richard and Susie basically treat me like a member of their family, in that they let me just hang out in their home without feeling like a guest. So I muck in, and they let me put their kids to bed and do the washing up and stuff. They just treat me in a normal way. I don't have to be on my best behaviour. I just can chill out and slob. They have allowed me to have a really special part in the upbringing of their children by letting me be a godmother and really letting me have a relationship with them, so that I really am a part of their lives. They're comfortable with me just hanging out. They once told me they were buying a new car, and one of them made the comment to the other, 'Oh, we must buy a car big enough for Ella to come too.' What's also great is that they don't tread on eggshells with regard to my singleness. They just behave like it's totally normal and not second best.

Jane:

[A friend in a family I knew] would take me shopping if she was going. The washing machines at my apartment cost money, and when she found that out she did my laundry every week. We worked out our timetables at college so that I could mind her kids when she was in class, as her husband worked. I was involved in the upbringing of their kids. They came to my graduation, as my family didn't fly out, and had a special dinner and cake for me, and presents. Their home was my home. For one holiday, they invited me to stay with them on this wonderful farm where the wife's grandparents live.

The husband, who passionately loves his wife, also knows how to make their female friends feel great. He is not afraid to compliment them and loves them like sisters. If a single girl needs to be reminded that she is loved and loveable, I say send her to him! They have three young lively kids and yet they structure the day around you, and get the kids in line with that idea too. We visited her grandparents in their smaller house on the farm and talked and talked. The grandfather pastors a small church; the next thing I knew, that church had enveloped me as well as my friends into their midst. There was no room or time to notice that I was single, or covet the life my [married] friends had, because I wasn't outside it watching them have a great holiday, I was with them having a great holiday.

I had to ask Jane if her friends were *really* that perfect?

> No. But they receive grace and so life is lived. And we talk
> about struggles and how marriage is hard, how parenting is
> hard. Tears are shed, but I am not left outside that. I am
> inside the family unit as far as they are concerned, so I see
> the reality of life, and so there is no sitting on the edge
> watching a seemingly perfect family. I know they are not
> perfect, but I'd be happy going on holidays with them any
> day. When they were moving to another country last year,
> their eldest (who was five) saw the apartment and he didn't
> understand where I was going to sleep. He just assumed I
> was going with them. I guess that shows how much they
> had drawn me into their family.

There are ways that married people and families can get it
wrong sometimes, too. Kate reflects on one of her more negative
experiences.

> I've got these married friends who are really lovely and
> kind, and they invited me round to watch a DVD with
> them, because they knew I had been feeling lonely lately.
> It was such a lovely idea, but when I got there I was
> sandwiched on the sofa between these two couples sitting
> on laps and cuddling, while we watched a soppy romance
> movie. I've never felt more single in my life! Their
> motivation for having me round was great, but I don't
> think they'd really thought through how that might have
> made me feel.

Physical touch
The way that couples behave physically with each other is a very
challenging but really key area in which they can love their single
friends well. The absence of everyday intimate physical touch
is one of the biggest deficits for a single person, and seeing it

exhibited by others all over the place exacerbates the pain. I am really grateful to godly couples who are sensitive enough to keep their hands off each other when they are with their single friends, while demonstrating their very real love for each other in different ways. I am surprised by the number of otherwise godly couples who seem to have a complete blind spot when it comes to showing consideration in this area. I am not suggesting that Christian couples should sit at opposite sides of the room and keep their hands firmly planted in their pockets whenever they have single guests, but there are levels of tactility that are less considerate and helpful. Mark talks about missing physical touch.

The absence of everyday intimate physical touch is one of the biggest deficits for a single person.

I'll be honest; I'm not a great fan [of singleness]. I can see advantages to it, in that you've got more time for God; you've got more time for other people. But equally there are downsides. I mean, as much the Holy Spirit is a great comforter, there are times when you really do wish you could have physical intimacy with someone else. And I'm not even talking about sex, but having someone close like a partner to share with. Silly things, like someone to cuddle up with in front of the TV and all that kind of thing, and obviously you miss that as a single person. It's perhaps even worse for me, because I've been in long-term relationships. I've had that, so it's something I've had and now don't have any more. So that is quite difficult to do without.

Particularly for someone struggling with same-sex intimacy issues, the area of physical touch can be a bit of a minefield. This can be a particular issue for girls, who tend to be much more comfortable with same-sex physical touch, so that the boundaries can be less clear. I asked Ruth to tell me about her experiences of this.

> Have I ever got things wrong with physical touch? Yeah, all the time! For instance, with my friend Anna; early on in our friendship, things were really awkward for me. She's very, very tactile with everybody, and it's not necessarily an issue for her, but at first I found it uncomfortable and unhelpful. For example, we were sitting on the bed once, and she hugged me and it lasted for ages. I ended up running off for a cigarette because I was scared of my feelings.
>
> *... the area of physical touch can be a bit of a minefield.*
>
> There was another time when we were lying on the bed and then it got cold, so we got into the bed, and it was emotionally confusing. I knew how to read it from her point of view – that it didn't mean what it might have meant if it was somebody else – but for me it wasn't very helpful. So we had a talk about it and we came up with some boundaries. I wouldn't go in her room when she stayed over, and we wouldn't hug loads. It was difficult, because there wasn't much physical contact at all for a while after that, but now we seem to have managed to get a happy medium, where she can hug me and I don't freak out! We have managed to get the balance right and I'm really grateful to Anna for being prepared to help me.

Ruth went on to explain how she tends to deal with confusing situations like the one she describes.

It's helpful if you've got the sort of friendship where you can be honest and talk about things. For example, when I talked with Anna, although it wasn't a particularly fun conversation to have, I was able to be honest about how I was getting confused about her, and it was fine. She seemed to understand, and she has talked to me about it since. She didn't seem to think, 'Ooh, that was embarrassing so we won't talk about that again.' She asks me what is helpful and what isn't and she also realizes it's important still to hug me and isn't afraid to do so. She wants to be able to be affectionate, because that's what she's like anyway, and also it's important for me to have friendships where people will hug me.

In the past when I've told people I'm gay or I've told them that at times I find things confusing – just to make them aware it can be difficult – some have freaked out and not hugged me at all, which is not a helpful response. I would like people to be normal around me and help me to have good friendships, and to recognize that the learning process involves making mistakes sometimes.

All of us need a healthy level of touch, but it can be confusing for a gay person to get this right. For me, it has felt as though touch is a language that everyone else seems to speak fluently, but I've never quite got the grammar. My need for touch is strong, but I know that what feels natural to me can sometimes be informed more by my distorted sexuality than by what is healthy. The differences and signals involved can be subtle, especially for girls. This is why Ruth describes the confusion that she felt in her

I would like people . . . to recognize that the learning process involves making mistakes sometimes.

friendship with Anna. Ruth went on to describe the kind of help needed to get past this.

> It's important to realize that one mistake doesn't have to mean the end of it all, or that you're never going to get it right. I need people who are happy to walk the journey with me, who are secure enough not to panic if I get something slightly wrong. Learning how to have wholesome friendships is like learning a musical instrument. It would be rubbish if you made one mistake and your teacher said, 'Oh, you won't be able to play the piano now, sorry. You've messed it up.' Good teachers always help you to work through your mistakes and get to the point where you're getting it right more often.

It's important to realize that one mistake doesn't have to mean ... that you're never going to get it right.

A great way to love and support your gay friend, then, is to be generous with the physical affection that they would otherwise miss out on (and that in many cases they will have seriously lacked in childhood),[4] but to do this sensitively and with grace and patience, as you learn together how to do it in a healthy way.

Church

Churches have a real opportunity and responsibility to look after the single members of their congregations. This is what Ruth sometimes finds difficult about church life.

I find 'family services' difficult, because they tend to involve nuclear families, often with children, which makes me feel like an excluded spectator. At Easter we were invited to come up for communion 'with our families'. I found that hard because my family live in another city and they're not yet Christians, so I was on my own.

I like to see the church as my family, even though I don't always feel very included. A lot of the ways that people get to know each other in church are through things like parents and toddlers groups and young mums' Bible studies. I also know lots of people who've benefited from courses for engaged couples and marriage-building courses, but there doesn't seem to be equivalent support for single people. The only things that I see for single people seem to be focusing on a goal of getting married, or groups catering for young singles, such as students. There doesn't seem to be much for long-term single people, to help them, to build them up and encourage them to make the most of it.

If we are to agree with the Bible and say that the single state is as much a blessing as being married, then the resources and support offered by the church ought to reflect that. Al Hsu, author of *The Single Issue*, highlights a possible reason why the church finds this difficult:

The history of Christian singleness has been that of a pendulum swinging back and forth between two equally unhealthy extremes. Jewish society elevated marriage and family to the extent that it marginalized the single person. Religious leaders were always married. Then New Testament Christian teaching raised singleness to an equal level with marriage. Then the early church influenced by Gnosticism, advocated an asceticism that taught singleness as the better way. Only worldly people married, while holy monks and nuns forsook marriage. In reaction to the abuses of enforced chastity, the Protestant Reformers rejected clerical celibacy and instead elevated marriage and family over singleness ... a truly Christian view of both singleness and marriage will honour both equally without disparaging one or the other. Recovering such a balance is the first step toward a church where singles are valued equally with marrieds.[5]

It is vitally important that churches preach that singleness is equal in value to marriage. In an interview between Al Hsu and John Stott, Stott said this:

If marriage is good, singleness is also good. It's an example of the balance of Scripture that, although Genesis 2:18 indicates that it is good to marry, 1 Corinthians 7:1 (in answer to a question posed by the Corinthians) says that 'it is good for a man not to marry'. So both the married and single state are 'good'; neither is in itself better or worse than the other.

... a truly Christian view of both singleness and marriage will honour both equally without disparaging one or the other.

If the Bible is clear, our attitudes in church ought to be clear too. The key way to do this is to avoid the trap of treating singleness as a temporary state that will be relieved by marriage: saying, in effect, that singleness while waiting to get married is equal to marriage, but has an expiry date. This underlying attitude is shown when churches have 'twenties and thirties' groups for their singles. There is then nowhere for singles over thirty-nine to fit in, within the church. Thirty-nine is the expiry date. A simple solution would be to give the singles group a more inclusive name. Once again, Al Hsu has an interesting insight here:

The singles group at my church is named Kairos. Kairos is one of the Greek words for time . . . a proper perspective for the single life is to see every day as a kairos moment: an opportunity for either good or evil. Christians are called to do our best to follow Jesus daily.

Maybe we can compare how we live our lives to how we watch films on our VCRs. Some people like to rewind, to replay good parts that have already gone past. Others want to fast-forward to parts that haven't happened yet. But films (and life) are best experienced when we let the tape play – without excessive use of rewind, fast-forward, pause or stop.

> Kairos *is one of the Greek words for time . . . a proper perspective for the single life is to see every day as a* kairos *moment: an opportunity for either good or evil.*

I love this mindset of thinking of singleness as a present opportunity, rather than a temporary stopgap. The word *kairos* embodies this attitude; one that would be so helpful in the church.

Leaving the scene

In Chapter 4 I outlined why the gay scene can be so important to gay people. For a person who has spent some time there before conversion, leaving the welcoming and liberating arms of the gay scene and moving into the Christian subculture can be difficult.

When I have been to a gay bar, it has had (personally) little to do with picking someone up. It has been a place where I know that the only people who will walk through the door will be women, so I can imagine I live in a world where men do not exist, which can seem so much easier. It has been a place where women can kiss other women and no one bats an eyelid or nudges and points or shouts abuse. It has been a place where I could sit with my girlfriend without worrying that our body language was giving us away. It has been a place where I would not have to worry about aggressive fallout if I were caught 'checking out' another woman. It has been a place where I can lay down my masks and be who I feel I really am. I can talk as loudly as I want about women I find attractive or experiences I've had, without worrying if someone will overhear me. It is a bubble where everything is as my sinful heart would like it to be and where everything feels so much easier.

Of course, to want to be in a place where I can indulge my sin in this way is wrong, but I can't deny the pull towards going to a place where I can feel this way. If you are straight, it can be hard to imagine how it might feel to have to go to a special place to be publicly physical with your partner, or to have certain conversations, or to feel that you are like everyone else.

Those kinds of feelings of belonging and shared identity are liberating and intoxicating.

Recently, I went to a gay bar after several years of staying away, and I enjoyed all of the feelings I've just described. Those kinds of feelings of belonging and shared identity are liberating and intoxicating. Even though the community that the church (ideally) offers is so much more real, it's not as immediate or exciting as the community that the gay scene offers. It was so tempting for me to get that 'fix' on my recent visit, but it had such a destructive effect on me. Thoughts like 'This is who I *really* am' and 'Why can't the world really be like this?' and 'Everything in my life is so hard and unfair; it's so much easier to live without denying my true self' came into my head after just one evening in one bar. Back at church, where people so often find it hard to be real with one another, the masks were back on, and I was once again in the secret minority. While striving for real relationships in a church setting is undoubtedly the right situation to choose, it is far less immediately appealing than the instant fix of the gay scene, however false a solution the latter might be.

The point I am making is that sex is not the only temptation that a Christian struggling with homosexual feelings has to face. There are places, as well as people, books, films, TV programmes and pictures, that are also best avoided. I am not encouraging legalism, but I do know that there are many things that can cause me to compromise in my own thinking. I am sure that anyone who has been single can relate to the feeling you get after watching a slushy romantic movie with a happy ending. Often it's not 'feel good' at all, but leads to aching loneliness and self-pity and to idolization of the romantic ideal. When we entered the cinema, we felt content. When we left, we wondered how we had ever endured the alien injustice of life without a boy/girlfriend!

. . . sex is not the only temptation that a Christian struggling with homosexual feelings has to face.

There are things that are helpful and things that are unhelpful. For a gay person, these things can be even more potent, and therefore more dangerous. This is not because the struggle is any less real for straight singles, but more because for gay people it is so tied up with seductive issues like identity. Seeing a film with gay characters, or going to a place where I know there will be plenty of gay people, makes me question not just whether I can cope with my single status, but whether I am denying my true self.

Leaving friends

One of the most painful consequences of leaving the gay scene behind is that often friends have to be left behind too. Mark shared his experience of this.

I've had to give up a lot of friends, and that's been difficult, because there are certain friends I have who just don't believe that I can make this kind of change. If I have any interaction with them, they're always wanting me to go out and saying, 'Why don't you get yourself another boyfriend?' and all this sort of stuff. So I've kind of had to stop a lot of contact and have given up a lot of friends. There are a few that I still have in my life and speak to, but I'm finding more and more that, as I tell them what my life is now and why I believe what I believe, they're kind of alienating themselves as well.

Because, you see, in a way I'm condemning their lifestyle. I try not to do it in a judgmental fashion, but the truth is, I owe it to them to warn them that the way they're living is not the right way. I've got a lot of unsaved friends, and the ones that I've tried to share the gospel with have usually taken offence and said, 'You've got on the Christian bandwagon and you're telling me that if I live like this I'm going to go to hell.' Well, basically, yeah, I am telling them that, if they don't repent and they don't accept Christ and they die without him, that's exactly what will happen. You can imagine that this has not gone down too well with a lot of my friends. So it has cost me a lot, and I do feel quite isolated in some respects.

There's another friend I've known for twenty years. Now he's a very promiscuous, very party-loving, gay guy. He really doesn't like what I've become. He thinks I've become some kind of religious maniac, obsessed with Christianity, and that I want to force it onto every gay man. He's been quite vocal in that, and so I see him hardly at all, whereas we used to hang out an awful lot. Having said that, it's probably a good job that I don't spend too much time with him, because he's very into the drug and sex side of the gay scene, and the chances are, if I hang out with him too much, I'd be tempted to go back into things that I shouldn't. But again, you're talking about a twenty-year friendship; it's difficult to give up.

I'll be honest: most people I've shared the way I feel with haven't really accepted it. And it's not just guys. I've got girlfriends who say, 'You're a fool to deny the way you are. You're just going to cause yourself grief, and who's to say that God didn't make you that way?' I had a long – almost – argument on the phone with a friend the other day about that very thing. She just can't accept that God would make me give all this up. So it's not easy, I'll be honest. But I've got support, and I've got God on my side.

Gay people are leaving behind a culture that had seemed so supportive and perhaps was the first place they had ever really fitted in.

This is a huge cost for some people, and perhaps it would not occur to many of us that this is something that someone might have to deal with on becoming a Christian. Gay people are leaving behind a culture that had seemed so supportive and perhaps was the first place they had ever really fitted in. Instead, they have to cut themselves off from their support networks and trust themselves to a new culture and a new group of people who can seem particularly hard to trust, because of the media representation of Christians.

A different world

Although I personally became a Christian after only just beginning to dip my toe into the gay scene,[6] I still found becoming a Christian a difficult culture shock. Sometimes, the longer we have been Christians, the more we forget how different we are from the rest of the world. I could not get used to all of these smiling, friendly people! This may sound strange, but I found it very difficult to trust anyone, because I thought everyone was fake. I knew that I was unhappy as a new Christian, because of all the new difficulties I was facing, so I couldn't understand why everyone else insisted on being so publicly joyful. I thought it was all a mask. I retreated from making friends or making myself vulnerable to anyone. Praying out loud was strange and scary, and all that singing was embarrassing. I had a whole new vocabulary to learn and an old – rather blue – one to lose. It was a big adjustment, and not one that I made very smoothly. How much more difficult must it be to make this adjustment with much to leave behind on the gay scene? Ruth had a similar experience.

Christian culture was a really hard thing for me to adjust to and still, ten years on, I find it really, really hard. I think it's because a lot of Christians are very different from me. As I've got older, a lot of them have got married and had children, and I feel there's an expectation to do the same, even if it isn't directly expressed. It seems that people don't really know what to do with you if you're not married, and there are ongoing difficulties with loneliness and building relationships that are meaningful but not sinful. A lot of Christians are from different backgrounds from me, especially if they have been brought up in Christian homes and never really been exposed to things like clubbing, drinking, drugs and sex. This makes it harder to explain my frustrations and difficulties to people, and most of them never ask about me and my background, my interests and my struggles.

... people don't really know what to do with you if you're not married ...

Stories like this are a reminder for us that not every Christian comes from a Christian home, and so the culture shift is more difficult than perhaps we realize. It also reminds us not to make assumptions about new Christians. I remember, when I first became a Christian, being in a conversation with a group of university-aged girls, and the assumption being that all present were virgins, I guess because young unmarried Christian girls usually are! But not always. Many people come to Christ from all kinds of backgrounds, and even those who have been brought up in Christian homes may have made mistakes in this area. Having this kind of mindset is helpful for all kinds of 'latecomers' to Christianity, not just those from a gay background. Our role must always be to show grace to people. We can never know what stories or struggles they may be hiding, until they let us into their lives.

For a gay person, making oneself vulnerable by coming out can be particularly scary.

Coming out

For a gay person, making oneself vulnerable by coming out can be particularly scary. Although I have done it countless times now, sometimes to whole rooms full of strangers, it still makes my knees wobble every time. It is important that, when someone comes out, friends handle the information in a sensitive way. Ruth talks about some of her own experiences.

While most of the Christians I have told haven't been openly hostile, the overwhelming reaction to me sharing my testimony or telling people about my sexuality has been fairly disappointing. Most people have been OK about it at the time, but haven't asked many questions or brought it up later. So there are a lot of people I've told who've never mentioned it again. It feels like a bit of a closed door because I've taken a step to be vulnerable, and now I don't feel like I could take the initiative to bring it up again.

Unfortunately, I have also been misunderstood on occasions. When I first joined the CU at university as a new Christian I had people who wanted to whisk me away for a weekend of intensive prayer ministry, and it frightened me because I didn't even know what that was. They weren't very sympathetic towards me, and I think the gay thing shocked them. They seemed to think I needed loads of prayer to 'cast it out' of me. With hindsight, I think it was quite an unhelpful reaction.

It's good for people to ask questions, so that they understand what you hope to achieve by sharing your story with them.

There are different levels of sharing, as well. Sometimes I tell people about my homosexuality because I'm really struggling and need help like prayer or counselling. Other times I'm simply sharing it as a piece of information because it might be useful: for example, when I've been doing evangelism with a friend and we've come across somebody who's gay, it has been helpful for me to share with my friend that I'm gay too. It's good for people to ask questions, so that they understand what you hope to achieve by sharing your story with them.

Thankfully, I do have some friends who have responded really well and been very supportive. They've asked questions and allowed me to talk about it on a more ongoing basis. Some people have even read books that I've lent them to help them understand my struggles, which I've found *really* helpful.

It is difficult to know how to handle the news if someone comes out just out of the blue, but the things that Ruth describes above are useful. Having the kind of open, mutually vulnerable, real relationship where friends feel they can safely share anything is an important start. If someone does say they are gay or struggling with their sexuality, not showing shock helps that person not to feel like a freak. However, if you genuinely *are* shocked by your friend's revelation, this too is a perfectly legitimate reaction to have. You are finding out something about a loved one that may cause you to question whether you ever really knew them.

There may be a sense of loss associated with this, and that is OK. It is important to respond to these feelings by trying to discover for yourself why this is your reaction, and then trying to come to terms with it. It is also important to explain to the person who has just come out to you that, although you need a bit of time to think things through, this does not mean that you are distancing yourself from them, but that you still love and care for them. Listening, asking questions and reassuring the friend that nothing has changed between you is the next step. Finally, treating the subject as one that can be revisited, without it being a constant obsession or a complete taboo, is helpful. Some of the time you may have to be the one initiating this, to reassure your friend that it is a safe subject to pursue.

Leaving lovers

By far the most painful and difficult thing that a Christian struggling with homosexuality can face is having to end a relationship because of what the Bible says. A friend supporting someone going through this should act just as they would with a friend who was suffering a break-up in a straight relationship. This may sound like an obvious point to make, but I have heard too many stories of friends being (often unintentionally) callous by assuming that because the break-up was so clearly *the right thing to do* that the person ought to be glad that the relationship was over. Of course, it is true that God is gracious in these situations, and a very real freedom often results, but the grief of a broken relationship is no less painful and raw.

In fact, the pain of a gay break-up is compounded by the fact that the relationship was begun (subconsciously) in the first place as an attempt to heal the same-sex deficits of childhood. Since the relationship is part of the person's reparative drive to meet those unmet needs, breaking it off can lead to feelings of hopelessness, desperation and even physical pain, as these wounds are left wide open once again. A lot of love and support is needed from Christians who can point them back to the healing love of Christ.

A close second to the pain of a break-up is having to say no to beginning a relationship where there is mutual attraction, perhaps leading to that friendship ending completely. It is when I have to do this that I find myself questioning my sanity most as a Christian. It seems so profoundly masochistic to meet someone I'm attracted to, find that the attraction is mutual, and then say no to it all. The most helpful thing that a friend did for me in this situation recently was to remind me of passages like Psalm 37. This psalm reminds us that righteousness often looks laughable in this life, while sinners seem to prosper wherever we look. The point of view described by the psalm is that God is not fazed by this. His perspective is certain, and there will come a time when the righteous will be proved correct in living that way. I really needed my friend to remind me gently of that perspective: that it is always right to do right, even when it looks like madness and hurts like anything. Often we need someone outside a situation to help us to regain this kind of perspective.

> ... righteousness often looks laughable in this life, while sinners seem to prosper wherever we look.

Most of the responses outlined in this chapter are fairly basic, helping us to be good friends to Christians in any situation. That is because, in most ways, gay people are just like anyone else: broken people in need of Christ and in need of support, to help them to take up their cross each day. We all have the privilege, the opportunity and the responsibility to live out being the body of Christ to one another, whatever our circumstances.

Wrong reaction, right reaction

Ruth says:

I didn't actively go looking for a relationship, but I met
Clare on a Christian project and we got on really well. She
told me that she was bisexual and I told her that I was gay,
so we knew quite early on, and I just thought it was great
that we could talk to each other about it. We had some
really honest conversations. However, quite soon it turned
into flirting, and I guess it boosted my self-esteem that
somebody liked me and found me attractive. At the end
of the project we ended up kissing, and then I had to go
home. Immediately I thought, 'That was a mistake;
I shouldn't have done that,' and I didn't want to pursue
things. But I missed her so much, and it felt unresolved.
It didn't feel like something that I could simply walk away
from. I suppose the strength of my feelings made me doubt
what the Bible said about homosexuality, as well. In
particular I didn't really know why it was wrong. I guess
I thought that as we were both Christians, and it didn't

involve anyone else, then maybe we could make it work. I also thought that if it was wrong, then it would go wrong or break down in some way. I thought it might become obvious why God said 'Don't do this', and then that would answer all my questions and doubts . . . I think I did think it was wrong deep down, but there were all sorts of complicated emotions and thoughts to work through.[1]

Inevitably, some of us will have friends who, although they call themselves Christians, still choose to pursue relationships with a member of the same sex. In this chapter, I want to explore three ways in which that might happen, and how we might deal with it as friends of those who begin a relationship of this type.

> . . . it is very difficult to know how to love someone well in a situation where a same-sex physical relationship has begun.

One way is for two people to have a full-blown sexual relationship, but there are also two other ways of 'practising' homosexuality. One is by having a non-sexual, but inappropriately intimate relationship with someone of the same sex. The third way to be explored here is to have an emotionally dependent friendship: a friendship that can cross appropriate boundaries of emotional and, sometimes, physical intimacy.

Dealing with friends who begin homosexual relationships

Since homosexual conduct is so clearly condemned in Scripture, it is very difficult to know how to love someone well in a situation where a same-sex physical relationship has begun. We need to work out how to do this, both communally as a church and individually as friends. The difficulty lies in the fact that one wants to continue showing love to the friend, while making it clear that one does not condone the behaviour. It is also a very delicate issue for church leaders to handle, as they try to strike the right balance between grace and discipline. Unfortunately, it is an area in which both churches and individuals often get it wrong, which has profound and far-reaching effects for those involved, as will be seen in the story of Ruth and Clare.

Part of the reason that we find it so hard to know how to respond is that we forget why such relationships start. We over-react, because we think that a person is committing the most flagrant sin, and therefore begin to jump to conclusions about their starting on the slippery slope to hell. It helps if we do not panic. It helps to remember the facts from Chapter 2: that this is just an illegitimate way to meet a legitimate need. It is worth repeating Andy Comiskey's helpful quote here:

When strugglers understand there's a normal and legitimate need at the core of their sexual tendencies, they find the truth liberating.

> The homosexual tendencies [the individual] faces are really red flag warnings that deeper, non-erotic needs are surfacing from the soul.
>
> When strugglers understand there's a normal and legitimate need at the core of their sexual tendencies, they find the truth liberating. They aren't perverts who love evil for evil's sake. An innocent, involuntary need is expressing itself in a broken way. That grants them the profound freedom to care for their needs while not submitting them to a false solution.[2]

This is not to say that the homosexual practice is excusable, but rather that it is not a sign that the Christian has lost all connection with the Holy Spirit and taken the first step on an irredeemable path. Often, people who begin relationships like this do so while wrestling with their conscience, but feel too weak to say no. Clare describes the initial reasons why she ended up pursuing a relationship with Ruth.

> My first argument was not terribly mature. I just really thought, 'It's so unfair! It's so rare for two people to actually like each other; why should we not be allowed to do something about this?' Most of my experiences of fancying people prior to that point had been one-sided, usually my fancying them. But suddenly here was somebody who I really fancied, who also fancied me, and that just seemed like too rare a thing to pass up really lightly. So I justified it to myself because I just couldn't let myself walk away from it.

Clare's reasoning, though she admits it was not the best, is easy to sympathize with. It is no small thing to walk away from a situation like this (as any straight Christian who has been attracted to a non-Christian will know). Adding this sympathy to the point made by Comiskey above (and to the truth that we are *all* capable of more sin than we dare to imagine) should lead to a response of compassion and patience, and a commitment to speaking the truth to our friends.

. . . we are all *capable of more sin than we dare to imagine . . .*

Sadly, this response is not often the one that gay people meet. Clare described to me some of the more negative reactions of her church friends when she began her relationship with Ruth.

There was just a load of rejection, lots of people not phoning me, not talking to me for months. Because I very quickly left church, I was soon not seeing a lot of friends, and nobody phoned me to say, 'Oh, I haven't seen you for a while; are you all right?' People 'outed' me to other people, so I then had no control over who did and didn't know. I told a leader from my previous church. He then told this other guy, and he then told a lot of other people in that church and in that whole friendship group. So stuff got back to me about other people that he told, and people would be saying things like, 'Oh, Clare, isn't she a lesbian? Did you hear this, this and this?' Whisperings that I would then get to hear. He was just so condemnatory, and I was only hearing it at third or fourth hand. I dread to think what he would actually have said if he'd had a chance to tell me what he thought.

Another friend – Fiona – really hurt me. She was a really good friend and we were really close, and I feel the whole thing has, in loads of ways, just ruined our friendship. She was a bit of a classic for being really understanding and listening, but sometimes being visibly shocked by the things I was telling her, which was not what I was needing. And never phoning, never e-mailing, never following up by actually being there. She'd be all 'Oh, this doesn't change a thing; we're still good friends', but then wouldn't live it out and wouldn't call me; wouldn't be there for me. It feels as if she doesn't really value our friendship.

I also feel like it's changed the way we relate to each other in our friendship, in terms of what she trusts me with in her life. We used to talk a lot about our views of life, the universe and everything, and share ideas and opinions, but I feel now she doesn't do that with me because she doesn't trust my input, because I'm this sinful person who does things that she wouldn't approve of, and so she wouldn't agree with my views on life. So that makes me feel really sad, because I feel like I've partially lost a really good friend. It's not the same.

This kind of testimony is painful to hear. Clare's story illustrates the consequences of gossip and indiscretion, as well as documenting her alienation when she was in need of so much support. Largely, these kinds of responses come from people who just don't know what to do with a situation like this, rather than from deliberate callousness. Clare's friend Fiona seemed somehow to stop seeing Clare as the person she once knew: a friend with struggles who needed support and Christian love. Now that Clare was struggling with this particular sin, Fiona began to relate to her completely differently. This was also perhaps the case for the other friends who stopped phoning. Clare was still the same person and needed to be treated and loved in the same way as before.

Clare was still the same person and needed to be treated and loved in the same way as before.

Often we are under the misconception, sometimes subconsciously, that if we are too nice to someone in a situation like this, they will think that we are condoning what they are doing. Jesus never approached anyone in this way, but always loved people back to repentance,[3] while never compromising on speaking the truth about sin. We ought to do the same. Clare went on to talk about a friend who did this well.

My friend Cat was completely amazing and remains amazing now. She was really supportive. She told me that she disapproved of what I was doing, which I really appreciated, because I didn't want her to lie to me and pretend that it was fine. But she did it in a really compassionate way, and she reaffirmed the fact that we were still friends and it did not change anything. She basically said, 'I really care about you; I really want you to be OK. I want the best for you. This isn't the best for you. I'm concerned about you; I'm worried about you; but I'm not going anywhere.' She's great in terms of just being there and listening. She's just great at quality time, and she didn't change that at all. In lots of ways, I've got to know her better during this. We were friends before, but not such good friends, I suppose, so it kind of strengthened our relationship. She's talked to me about personal things that I know she doesn't talk to other people about, so it's an ongoing reciprocal friendship which I really value. She really stands out as amazing.

Cat sounds brilliant! She did all the right things. She did not tell Clare that what she was doing was right. She was clear that she believed it was wrong, but said this in the context of the fact that she cared about Clare and wanted the best for her. She also continued to treat Clare like Clare and offered her all the support she needed. If all of us behaved like Cat, people like Clare would have a much safer environment, should they decide to end things in their own time as a response to the conviction of the Holy Spirit. Clare would have a circle of loving friends to help fill the gap left by her lover. If her only experience had been of those people in the previous story, there would have been no one left to support her. Obviously this reaction is the ideal, but it is important to bear in mind the

... she reaffirmed the fact that we were still friends and it did not change anything.

comments made in the 'Coming out' section of Chapter 5: that the most important thing is to be honest about how you feel initially when reacting to news like this. However, the more a friend can create ongoing support like Cat's, the better.

Meeting partners

One situation where this becomes difficult to live out is when your friend wants you to meet their partner. This is a difficult issue to get right. For a long time I refused to meet the partners of Christian gay friends. This decision was partly informed by wanting to protect my own vulnerabilities: I knew it was not helpful for me to see two people of the same sex together in that way. It was also partly because of the mistaken view (mentioned above) that if I met the partner I would be 'encouraging' the relationship. I thought that by meeting them I would automatically be perceived as condoning it. Having spoken to a few friends about how this made them feel, I have now changed my thinking.

> *I thought that by meeting them I would automatically be perceived as condoning it.*

Ruth said this:

While we were going out, there were some people who hung around with Clare and me and invited us to things. I didn't know whether that was a wise thing to do from a Christian point of view, but I certainly needed friends and appreciated people being nice to me. I used to think that it wasn't a good idea to invite people's partners to things because it might look like you're condoning the relationship. However, when I was in a relationship and people still wanted to be with me and Clare, it didn't make me think 'Oh, well, it's OK to go out with Clare now!' It didn't make me think that people were endorsing our relationship, but it made me realize that some Christians do love me. So I think, as long as people are clear, then it is a really helpful thing to do.

Ruth's comment about realizing she was loved because her friends were willing to meet Clare is really helpful. As long as we are clear and consistent in ensuring our friend never hears us as condoning the relationship, it speaks volumes to show someone that they are still loved and accepted even while they are struggling with sin.

> . . . it speaks volumes to show someone that they are still loved and accepted even while they are struggling with sin.

The church leader: tough decisions, huge consequences
Church leaders have a challenge to face when someone in their congregation begins a gay relationship. I asked a Church of England vicar what he would do in this situation.

First of all, there is the attitude of the heart: if someone hates what they're doing. We're all sinful. It's also a case of: do they think a particular action – in this case homosexual sex – is wrong, or do they think that it's OK? But Jesus is quite clear about the way that we should exercise discipline: 'If your brother sins against you, go and show him his fault, just between the two of you. If he listens to you, you have won your brother over. But if he will not listen, take one or two others along, so that "every matter may be established by the testimony of two or three

witnesses''. If he refuses to listen to them, tell it to the
church; and if he refuses to listen even to the church, treat
him as you would a pagan or a tax collector.' [Matthew
18:15–17] So there's a three-step process.

This is of course the correct biblical procedure for dealing with
this situation, or any that requires church discipline: examining the
motivation of the heart, and going through the correct process in
the light of the findings. However, it is *so* important to do this with
much compassion and patience. Clare described the hurtful way
that her church responded when she admitted to them that she had
begun a relationship with Ruth.

I felt like I had to be honest with them, because I didn't feel
that I could sit in their church services and pretend it
wasn't happening, so I told them. They said, 'OK; you've
got one week. If in a week's time you haven't split up with
her, we're going to exclude you from membership, which
means you can't come to house group, or any prayer
meetings. We can't stop you coming on Sunday mornings.
So we'll exclude you from membership and tell the whole
church why.'
The house group thing especially seemed extremely
cruel. If I'm going to work this out, and if I'm going to
work this out with God, I need to be in a place where I can
talk to him, and have some other people who are going to
be nice to me while I do that. And so that was the thing
I felt like they were taking away from me the most, the
possibility of being part of a group. It didn't take me a
week to decide: I was leaving. I thought, 'That's that. I'm
not going to split up with her in a week. I'm not going to
do all these things. Bye-bye.' Although they'd told quite a
lot of other people in leadership, nobody else ever said
anything. I never had a conversation with any of those
people. Which makes it worse, that they know all these

> things about me, and I've never told them, and they've
> never even spoken to me about it.

I asked Clare how the church might have treated her differently.

> I wish they'd treated me like a human being, and not like a
> problem. I guess that's the main thing, that the whole spirit
> of their reaction to me was totally dehumanizing and failed
> to recognize that I'm a human being with feelings. I wish
> they'd just been a bit more laid back about things like
> timescale. The fact that I was
> given a week to decide to
> split up with somebody is
> just a hugely short period of
> time. I don't think anybody
> could make that kind of
> decision in a week. It seemed
> hugely unreasonable and
> really showed that they
> didn't understand what was
> going on. What *is* it
> reasonable to ask somebody
> to do in a week? Easy things
> happen in a week. It takes a
> long time to do difficult
> things. I guess I felt like they
> didn't make any real effort to understand *me*. Literally, I was
> a problem and I just needed squashing and dealing with, and
> they weren't prepared to let me deal with it in my own time
> and wrestle with it in my own way.

... their reaction to me was totally dehumanizing and failed to recognize that I'm a human being with feelings ... I was a problem and I just needed squashing and dealing with ...

I do not envy anyone having to make pastoral decisions in this
kind of situation. It must be so difficult to make the right call
between being firm with the truth of the Bible and being clear and
uncompromising on that, and at the same time judging the right

amount of time to show grace and to allow for the fact that this is a painful and confusing situation for someone to be in. It is a monstrously difficult call, but the consequences can be damaging if a situation is misjudged. I went on to ask Clare how the way she had been treated in her situation had affected her view of God.

> I think God's pretty horrible. I think it's very difficult to distinguish between God, church and Christians, particularly Christians in church leadership, because although they don't verbally claim to be God, they stand for God to such a huge extent that it's just really difficult to separate the two. So when Christians are horrible to me, it feels like God's horrible to me. So I feel like God's just a sadistic, abusive, violent, horrible being, who wants to torture, reject and hate me. I don't want to know somebody who's like that. Why would anyone want to know somebody who's like that?
>
> So the whole thing has *hugely* affected my view of God. It's obviously also affected my view of Christians, because how could it not? It makes me feel that a lot of them are brainwashed and brainwashing, person-denying, horrible and procedure-driven. Not understanding, just saying, 'This is a problem; this is how we deal with it', carrying through sets of procedures. I know that's not true of every Christian, because I do know some Christians who are not like that, but it makes me feel really excluded from this kind of happy-clappy little club of people who can be really sanitized and conforming.

This is such a heart-breaking testimony. It is the result of someone coming up against a lot of Christians who probably sincerely believed that they were doing the right thing, but seemed to have removed the person from the problem. They perhaps panicked and over-reacted, because homosexuality is viewed as such an enormous sin, and as a result failed to look beyond the surface to the glaring needs of a person. If the person concerned is consistently unrepentant and shows no desire to change, even after much patience has been shown, then of course the right thing must be to ask that person to leave. The section in 1 Corinthians 5 subtitled in the NIV as 'Expel the Immoral Brother!' is clear that this expulsion must come when the sexually immoral person is unrepentant: 'And you are proud!' (verse 2). So expelling someone from church must be the absolute last resort, as so many may be won back if they are consistently loved, listened to and understood. Ruth had a much more positive experience in her own church.

My minister came round to see me after I'd told him about the relationship and asked if I could talk to him about it.
It was an encouraging conversation and he seemed to understand the issues pretty well. He said that while I was still working things through, I could continue to be a church member, and be in the worship team and house group. However, if I decided to stay in the relationship long-term, then I would need to leave the worship team and resign my membership. I agreed with this approach and thought that was a really sensible thing to say. Although he didn't actually define what long-term meant, I thought his attitude to membership and the way he responded to my struggles was very good. As a person of integrity, I would have resigned my membership anyway, had I continued seeing Clare, as I knew my church

> *. . . expelling someone from church must be the absolute last resort, as so many may be won back if they are consistently loved . . .*

was part of the Evangelical Alliance, and it wouldn't have been appropriate for me to carry on being a member had I decided to stay with her.

In contrast to Clare, this is how Ruth viewed God after everything was over.

It has made me realize that I am capable of the most appalling rebellion against God, and that to resist the temptations, and stand any chance of doing the right thing, I need to be totally dependent on God. I think I've realized the importance of guarding my heart as well, and not allowing myself to be seduced by anything that's a counterfeit of real love. It can look very similar: caring about Clare and loving her wasn't wrong, but allowing that to become a sexual relationship wasn't God's best for either of us. At the time, it looked like Clare was someone who would stay in my life for the long term, and who I could have physical touch and companionship with, and who would know me and want to be with me. That's something that most people want.

It's shown me how deep God's forgiveness is, and how totally unworthy I am to receive it . . .

But it's such a lie that that's the way to get it. I need to be *so* aware that the devil is using every trick in the book to make me make that mistake again. It's also shown me how deep God's forgiveness is, and how totally unworthy I am to receive it, and yet it's there because of Jesus. Ultimately it's made me realize how much he loves me and how much I love him as well.

Of course, Ruth's relationship with God, as compared with Clare's, is not *just* indicative of the way that they were treated by their churches – personal choice and the state of their individual hearts are key[4] – but the support (or lack of it) from their churches will have had a huge impact on their long-term walks with the Lord. I know far too many stories similar to Clare's, where struggling Christians have been so hurt by their church and other Christians that they now really struggle to carry on with God. My plea is for extra compassion and patience to be applied in these situations, for the roots of loneliness and historic relational problems to be addressed by the church (rather than panicking over the homosexual fruits), and for people to be treated as people and not just as problems.

My plea is for extra compassion and patience . . .

Practising without practising

Gay Christians do not have to be having a full-blown relationship with someone to be sinning homosexually. There are a couple of other ways of relating that need to be explored.

One that I have come across is when two people of the same sex are enjoying a 'going out' relationship without having sex. Their argument is that the Bible condemns homosexual sex, so there is nothing wrong with them indulging in intimate things like kissing. I have to admit that my first response to people who say this is scepticism that they are actually not having sex. Sexual self-control is hard enough for heterosexuals who are going out, but if things get serious they at least have marriage to look forward to. If two gay people reach the same level of commitment and intimacy, they have only a frustrating future of abstinence ahead of them. If they *have* managed not to give in sexually, then I do not envy them the constant battle for self-control. It is clearly much harder *not* to have sex if you are kissing someone you are attracted to, than if you are not doing this at all! So my first question would be whether or not this kind of relationship is practically sustainable in the long term.

My second response would be to point them to parallel situations where the morality is much easier to spot. For example, the Bible does not condemn kissing for heterosexuals either. However, if I were married to a man and discovered that he had been kissing another woman, I would not be reassuring my husband that he was free to do this according to the Bible! It would be a completely inappropriate level of intimacy for him to have with another woman. This is biblically implicit rather than explicit, for both the heterosexual and the homosexual situations, but that does not mean in either case that it is to be ignored.

The same grace, sensitivity and patience need to be applied in this situation as with a full-blown relationship . . .

Both of these points may seem very obvious to someone on the outside of the situation, but the fact is that a couple will have tried to contrive this biblical loophole (saying that the Bible does not condemn kissing) only because of a strong desire to be with someone. The same grace, sensitivity and patience need to be applied in this situation as with a full-blown relationship, however absurd and weak the reasoning may seem to us.

Emotional dependency

A different relational problem needing to be explored in this chapter is emotionally dependent relationships. I think I must have been in at least one emotionally dependent relationship for most of my life, seeing nothing wrong with this until I found out what 'emotional dependency' was. To me, it was a normal way of relating. Lori Rentzel[5] defines emotional dependency in the following way:

> Emotional dependency occurs when the ongoing presence and nurturing of another is believed to be necessary for personal security.

Such relationships are not only had by people struggling with homosexuality. This unhealthy element can be present in heterosexual friendships, romantic relationships and marriage, as much as between two people of the same sex. Heterosexuals can also experience it with members of the same sex, with little or no physical element involved, but it can also lead on to unexpected physical homosexual feelings. Jen and Karen, both heterosexual Christians, describe the characteristics that led them to realize that they were in emotionally dependent friendship with other girls.

First Jen:

I think I had to admit I was in an emotionally dependent friendship when I realized I wanted to spend every single moment of my time with her. Some of the warning signs were when I got really jealous of anyone else spending time with her. I'd also get annoyed and hurt if she'd told other people personal stuff before she'd told me. Our friendship was also quite physical, so we would hold hands and spend a lot of our time hugging. It was also really hard to say goodbye when we had to go, and I felt like I never wanted to leave her and always wanted to know when I would see her again; to know when the next fix was coming.

Now Karen:

There was a real intensity and a desire for exclusivity. I don't think I ever consciously thought 'Oh, I don't want anyone else to be involved', but I just never really wanted anyone else to be involved! There was an addictive element to it. So we spent loads and loads of time talking to each other, and with each other, and communicating with each other, and it just never felt like enough time.

However many hours we'd been talking, it would seem too short. Or however often we'd spoken, it would seem like we needed to speak again.

I lost interest in other friends, so even when I was with other people, I wasn't ... interested in talking to anybody unless it was her.

So there's the addictive element, and there was also probably a flattery element: ending up spending quite a lot of time telling each other how great we thought the other was. Also, when I wasn't talking to her, then I would be with other people and realize that I was often talking about her, or thinking about her, even when I wasn't with her. I lost interest in other friends, so even when I was with other people, I wasn't really interested in talking to anybody unless it was her. So even people who were very important to me actually didn't really *seem* very important to me.

Physical element

One particular problem with this type of friendship is that, although it can remain entirely emotional, it can be so all-consuming and obsessive that a sexual or physical element can often enter into it, even if the person in question normally relates entirely heterosexually. This can be an alarming discovery for some, as Karen describes.

I felt an amazingly strong physical compulsion to just be with her if I wasn't with her, if I knew I could. So if I was in the same building but not in the same room, I'd want to be in the same room. Then, when I was with her, I felt a compulsion to touch her or hug her. It felt physical, but it didn't feel particularly sexual, but I think it then *became* sexual. I found it very confusing and quite scary, because I wasn't really expecting it. It made me question my sexuality and identity, but I think to some degree I also enjoyed it. I found it hard because, as a Christian, I didn't believe that I should act on it, but I still enjoyed feeling attracted, and the sense of mutual attraction. But I found it quite frightening that I was considering things sexually that normally I wouldn't consider, and that I was considering them quite positively.

A healthy relationship is free and generous . . . While healthy friendship is joyful and up-building, emotional dependency produces bondage.

Lori Rentzel's booklet has a very helpful section that unpacks the difference between a friendship that is healthy and one that has become emotionally dependent:

There are some significant differences in a healthy friendship. A healthy relationship is free and generous. Both friends are eager to include others in their activities. They are happy when one friend hits it off with another person. In a good friendship, we desire to see the other reach his or her full potential, developing new interests and skills. In healthy relationships, we are affected by the things our friends say and do, but our reactions are balanced.

On the other hand, a dependent relationship is ingrown, creating mutual stagnation and limiting personal growth. A casual remark from our friend can send us into the heights of ecstasy or the pits of grief. When a close friend moves away, it is normal for us to feel sorrow and a sense of loss; but if one of the partners in a dependent relationship moves, the other is gripped with anguish, panic and desperation. While healthy friendship is joyful and up-building, emotional dependency produces bondage.[6]

It is easy to see how this type of friendship is inappropriate, but it is also a completely exhausting way of relating. Being so engrossed in another person means that eventually all your feelings of self-worth, even your mood, are dependent on the way your friend responds to you. It can make you behave in a completely irrational and exaggerated way. Steve recalls:

I'm a fairly balanced person in many areas of my life, but sometimes in these sorts of friendships I've behaved in ways I never normally would. It's a reaction to rejection or thinking you're going to lose that person. I remember one situation; the lad I was keen on had a girlfriend and I got extremely jealous and angry. Loads of emotions welled up that caused me to want to break them apart. It's actually very ungodly, the emotion that you feel. It's a very selfish way of relating to someone; wanting to possess them. When the guy I liked got a girlfriend, I was very aloof and was very offhand with the partner, ignoring her, not mentioning her name, basically pretending she didn't exist.

I remember one day we were at the pub. My friend was really annoyed with me because I'd ignored her and was giving her a vibe that I wasn't keen on her being there. My friend picked up on that and had a go at me – rightly so. I was trying to get between the two people, which caused real tension between my friend and me. I tried to get between them when they were walking off, I physically tried to muscle in, which was really bad. That's certainly not the way I would normally behave but it's a reaction to being really hurt.

It lasts for a long time, even when you come to terms with it and you actually understand what's happening. It's quite alarming when you discover what's going on. I was flabbergasted. It's taken about four or five years to deal with it and I still have an occasional problem with it.

Idolatry

In my own friendships, I have often begun to recognize the signs of emotional dependency creeping in. Even when I have become aware of what is happening, of the unhealthy elements and of the potential for things to become physical or sexual, I have still often been reluctant to give the friendships up. The sense of need in these friendships is difficult to express. If I couldn't have a proper romantic or sexual relationship, I badly wanted to have the next best thing: this 'special'

> Idolatry occurs whenever you place something higher in your heart than God.

friendship, where I could still feel that I was the most important person in someone's life; that they needed me and I needed them. It was easy to persuade myself that this was 'just friendship' and so it wasn't sinful. The truth is, however, that these types of friendship are idolatrous.

Idolatry occurs whenever you place something higher in your heart than God. Jeremiah 2:13 says:

My people have committed two sins:
They have forsaken me,
    the spring of living water,
and have dug their own cisterns,
    broken cisterns that cannot hold water.

This is a vivid description of what we are in reality doing, when we choose something else above God. It is as foolish as giving up living water in favour of drinking out of a cracked toilet bowl. The fact that I was not initially prepared to end these friendships, even though I knew where they were potentially heading, means that I was choosing this person over God's obvious will for me. The all-consuming nature of the friendships meant that I was frequently capable of letting down other friends, spending money I didn't have, skipping church and acting in very ugly, manipulative ways, just to be with – or win the favour of – my special friend. This is clearly putting someone else before God, and the right thing to do, at least for a period of time, is often to end the friendship.

Lori Rentzel highlights some reasons why this can be hard to do:

> Even when both parties realize a relationship is unhealthy, they may experience great difficulty in breaking the dependency. Often those involved will begin to separate, only to run back to each other. Even after dependencies are broken, the effects may linger on for some time. Let's look at some reasons why these attachments are so persistent.
>
> First, as painful as dependency is, it does give us some gratification. There is emotional security – a dependent relationship gives us the sense that we have at least one relationship we can count on and that we belong to someone. Our need for intimacy, warmth and affection might be filled through this relationship. And our egos are boosted when someone admires or is attracted to us. We also enjoy feeling needed...

The culture we live in has taken the truth 'God is love' and turned it around to mean 'Love is god'.

The second reason we find it hard to break dependent relationships is that we can't see them as sinful. The culture we live in has taken the truth 'God is love' and turned it around to mean 'Love is god'. Romantic or emotional love is viewed as a law unto itself. When you love someone (which means having intense romantic feelings for someone), anything you do with that person is okay. Viewed in this light, dependent relationships seem beautiful, even noble, especially if there is no overt sexual involvement. Genuine feelings of love and friendship might be used to excuse the intense jealousy and possessiveness present in the dependency.

Even when I know that I am in a friendship that is inappropriate in this way, I find it very hard to make the choice to end things. It is like the sailors in Greek mythology. They were experienced and would never normally have gone near dangerous rocks. However, many were lured into dangerous waters by the sirens. Even though the sailors knew the sirens meant evil, they could not resist their beauty and their seductive voices, so they met their deaths dashed on the rocks.

One of the reasons such friendships are so difficult to break is the amount of self-deception involved.

Emotionally dependent relationships (whether between heterosexual or homosexual people), like homosexual romantic or sexual relationships, are indicative of deeper unresolved issues. Many of the issues will be similar to those that lead to more obviously homosexual tendencies. Those who are entrenched in – or prone to – emotionally dependent relationships need to seek God's counsel in prayer as to what these roots might be in their case. Until these roots are dealt with, the pattern will continue.

How to help
In addition to addressing the root issues, friends of those currently enslaved in this kind of relationship can help in the following ways:[7]

- Encourage your friend to be honest with him- or herself, with God and with you. One of the reasons such friendships are so difficult to break is the amount of self-deception involved. The more a person tries to persuade themselves that a relationship is healthy and legitimate, the more likely it is to develop in an unhealthy way, and the less easy it is to be honest with others.
- Help your friend as *the friend decides* to separate gradually from the unhelpful relationship. You will most likely need to help with this, as self-deception will once again creep in and will give your friend excuses to stay in contact. There are times when it is appropriate to break off the relationship quickly rather than gradually: for instance, if sexual sin has occurred, or there is very obvious imminent potential for it. It is very important that the decision to end the friendship should come from the person involved, not from you. Of course you can warn, suggest and pray, but unless the decision has come from a genuine conviction of the heart by the Holy Spirit, any attempts at separation are likely to fail, because the temptation for reconciliation will be so great.
- Prepare to support your friend long-term. A separation is extremely painful. Allow your friend to grieve the loss, and resist the temptation to think that they ought to be pleased to be freed from sin. Encourage them to cultivate other non-dependent friendships, to help fill some of the immediate social gaps left from having spent the majority of time with one person. These friendships will also prove invaluable in the healing process, as they can help to teach your friend how to relate to others healthily, although this

can be a long and steep learning curve if emotional
dependency has been a lifelong relational habit.

- Finally, watch yourself! ('Brothers, if someone is caught in
  a sin, you who are spiritual should restore him gently. But
  watch yourself, or you also may be tempted' – Galatians
  6:1.) One of the powerful elements that can start this type
  of friendship is a 'need to be needed'. If you are helping a
  friend get through their relational struggles, the friend
  may rely on you, and you may find that you really enjoy
  this sense of being needed. It can in fact be powerfully
  addictive.

I can remember when I was helping a friend who was struggling
with sexuality issues. She had been worried about sharing her
struggles with her family and had been calling me frequently to seek
reassurance and perspective. One
day she called to say that her
family had accepted her and had
been really supportive. She was
over the moon! She made a
throwaway comment about not
needing to hassle me on the
phone all the time any more. I
told her how pleased I was that
things had gone well, but as soon
as I put the phone down I felt
devastated. I was horrified with
myself that I would actually want my friend to struggle, just so that
she would continue to need me, but I had to admit that this was
what I was feeling. This was a loud alarm bell for me that I was in an
ugly, unhealthy, emotionally dependent relationship, and it had
started because I had wanted to help someone.

So be careful when you are in a position to help someone.
Watch your own motives and feelings and, if necessary, ask
yourself whether someone else might be in a better position to

*Prepare to support
your friend long-term.
A separation is
extremely painful.*

help your friend, however indispensable he or she might make you feel.

Breaking off
Making the decision to end the friendship, or to take a long break away, seeking counselling and help in the interim,[8] though incredibly painful, can have very real fruits, as Jen and Karen describe.

Jen says:

It felt horrible, because I had to pull back from something that I really wanted. I felt like I couldn't live without her and stopping something as strong as that was really hard and painful. Also, I was pulling back from something that felt like it should be so right, because it's friendship and we're told that friendship is a really good thing. So it felt very unnatural to end it. Ending friendship, or trying to change a friendship to become a healthy one, is challenging, because you have really to test out the theory that God is enough, and that he is sufficient for our needs and will provide for us. But through it all I think I did get freedom, which was freedom from the weirdness that comes from being jealous and clinging on to each other all the time. So I was free to love other people well, as opposed to just wanting the attention of one person.

> *Making the decision to end the friendship, or to take a long break away ... can have very real fruits ...*

And I did sometimes discover that God really was enough. Not that I felt that every moment: there was pain and hurt as well, and there still is sometimes. But there was a freedom in bringing that pain to God and seeking him as the source of my needs and love, rather than another fallible human. Through it all I think I've been taught by God his way of loving, which is free and open and inclusive, rather than the selfish kind of loving which revolves around me.

And Karen:

When we ended it, it felt really right. I was really convinced that it was right. But it also felt really wrong and really painful. I think it just feels so unnatural to separate from someone that you love so intensely, especially when somebody seems to fit into your life so completely. It's quite scary to face life without that person and without that relationship. I found it difficult talking to non-Christians about it, who thought that it was just a crazy thing to do, because they thought that if you love someone, you should be with them regardless of any other considerations. I suppose I liked it when it felt right, and I didn't like it when it felt wrong, so I had to make a conscious decision that I was basing the decision, and my life, not only on how I feel but on what's right. That was a real help, and it meant that I could take it to God, even when it felt horrible. Especially

There was a real sense of freedom and joy in being obedient and in deliberately choosing Christ . . .

when it felt horrible. But it did feel right as well as wrong; quite extremely both.

The positive benefits were that it *was* right. There was a real sense of freedom and joy in being obedient and in deliberately choosing Christ above an idol. I had a clear conscience before God and a clear conscience with my Christian friends. I think just an *actual* freedom. To start with I didn't feel that free, because I was just so conscious of Kate. But as time passed, I did feel more and more free. Also, just not having that relationship consuming my time and my energy and my thoughts and my emotions meant I just had *loads* of time and energy to invest in other people and other relationships, and I needed to invest in them really. I think, also, I just got a right perspective on emotional dependency: that there is life beyond it or outside it, because it had just been so all-consuming in some ways. So freedom I guess is the main one. A big thing also is the conviction that what I had done was right for me, but it was also right for Kate, and that actually it was the most loving thing that I could have done for her.

Revisiting the siren analogy, Orpheus managed to avoid death from the sirens by singing more beautifully than they did and drowning them out. Part of what is needed to overcome such bondage is to seek God all the more strongly. If we sing God's song, then even the most beautiful song of the world will pale into insignificance.

Dealing with the mess and pain of relationships is so difficult: for the people involved and for those trying to support them. The wonderful truth is that we have a relational God who understands our feelings, however warped and selfish they may have begun to be. He does actually sympathize with us and understand: 'For we do not have a high priest who is unable to sympathise with our weaknesses, but we have one who has been tempted in every way, just as we are – yet was without sin' (Hebrews 4:15).

Wonderfully, he is also committed to changing and sanctifying us, so that we can learn new ways of relating, and become more and more like our Saviour himself. 'And we, who with unveiled faces all reflect the Lord's glory, are being transformed into his likeness with ever-increasing glory, which comes from the Lord, who is the Spirit' (2 Corinthians 3:18). If we were not Christians, we would be hopelessly in the bondage of these broken ways of relating and we would have no way of helping ourselves. We are not helpless; we are able to choose what is right: 'For sin shall not be your master, because you are not under law, but under grace' (Romans 6:14). We must help one another as we choose what is right; as we seek to serve God here and now by fighting for healthy friendships that glorify him, and by storing up treasures for ourselves in heaven that far outweigh our struggles now (Matthew 6:19–20).

Wonderfully . . . we can learn new ways of relating, and become more and more like our Saviour himself.

Commissioning

I wanted to write this book for people who love their gay friends
and want to love them well. If you are one of those people, I am
excited. My prayer is that what you have read will make an impact
on the way you live. If my prayer is answered, it will mean that you
can now love your friends – whether they are Christians or not yet
Christians – with informed compassion. You can also educate
others, having compassion on those who do not yet fully understand the issues. It will also mean that, as the number of Christians
with this kind of understanding grows, there will be wide-reaching
repercussions: There will be a greater number of non-Christian
homosexuals who will get to hear the gospel sensitively. There will
be fewer newspaper reports about bigoted, homophobic Christians.
There will be more Christians struggling with their sexuality who
will have at least one friend who understands them better and
so will help them to feel less lonely, isolated, afraid of being known,
or confused about their identity. What an exciting prospect!

There are a few key things I would like to remind you of as you
get stuck into living this stuff out, all of them rooted in a book
eternally better than this one.

All have turned away,
   they have together become worthless;
there is no-one who does good,
   not even one.
(Romans 3:12)

The gospel is a great leveller. It shows us, without compromise, that all of us have fallen short of God's standards. We need to be reminded of this sobering diagnosis, because we are quick to point the finger at one another and construct our own hierarchy of sin. For those who do not struggle with homosexuality, it helps to remember that any one sin is as shocking and disgusting to God as any other. For those of us who do struggle with it, it helps to remember that we are not the bottom of the pile; we are just as redeemed and perfect, through the received righteousness of Christ, as any other Christian. Alleluia!

He heals the broken-hearted
   and binds up their wounds.
(Psalm 147:3)

God does not look down on those who wrestle with their sexuality without compassion. He is a healing God, and he is the only one who can offer us lasting healing that glorifies him. There are roots and reasons for the way that sexuality develops. God knows and understands all the complexities of this and can work to heal and change us. The degree of this change will be different for each person, but God has promised that he is committed to our ongoing sanctification in every area of our lives. Remind your

> *He is a healing God, and he is the only one who can offer us lasting healing that glorifies him.*

friends of this, and that even our struggles are instrumental in it: 'Consider it pure joy, my brothers, whenever you face trials of many kinds, because you know that the testing of your faith develops perseverance. Perseverance must finish its work so that you may be mature and complete, not lacking anything' (James 1:2–4).

Be completely humble and gentle; be patient, bearing with one another in love.
(Ephesians 4:2)

We must also be prepared for the long haul. Many of these patterns of relating are lifelong learned. Most of them are literally emotional survival tactics; they will not be broken overnight. This is hard for both the person struggling with their sexuality and the supporting friend. The person struggling will find it hard to keep a perspective as victory seems to elude them. The friend will have to fight thoughts of 'Not again!' or 'Why doesn't he just end the relationship? It's so clearly the right thing to do!' We all need to respond by stepping outside our culture of instant fixes and hearing the Bible's call for us all to be patient with one another, as the Spirit changes us to 'live a life worthy of the calling you have received' (Ephesians 4:1).

We all need to respond by stepping outside our culture of instant fixes and hearing the Bible's call for us all to be patient with one another . . .

God sets the lonely in families . . .
(Psalm 68:6)

Being community-minded is one of the most important ways that any of the ideas in this book can be put into practice.

Homosexuality is not a problem only for the individuals who struggle with it; it is a problem for the church as a body. When one part of the body is hurting, the pain is felt all over it. Andrew Goddard makes this point in *Homosexuality and the Church of England*:

> If we are to have a Christian discussion, those of us for whom the 'issues' are not directly personal – the overwhelming majority – must take time to get to know gay Christians. In the words of Stephen Fowl: 'It should not, then, be the responsibility of homosexual Christians to provide "narratives of homosexual holiness" ... The onus is on other Christians who may enter (or have already entered) into friendships with homosexual Christians ...'[1]

All of us need to understand the issues. All of us need to engage with those who are actually struggling with the issues. All of us need to live lives that actively support those who struggle. The benefits of all of these can be reaped in the whole church.

When Jesus landed and saw a large crowd, he had compassion on them, because they were like sheep without a shepherd.
(Mark 6:34)

Compassion is a word that I have used again and again in every chapter. There are a number of Christians who can quote Scripture to explain exactly what the Bible says about homosexual practice. There seem to be far fewer who can couple this with real compassion for the people involved. This is a human issue, not just a theological one. In respect of our evangelism, too, we must not see the gay community as a group of unreachable, vocal and different people, living lives that fly in the face of biblical morality. They are in reality broken people, with mistaken identities, in desperate need of a Saviour.

**The night is nearly over; the day is almost here. So let us
put aside the deeds of darkness and put on the armour
of light.**

(Romans 13:12)

For those of us who struggle with our sexuality, living according to
the Bible is about as countercultural as you can get. Often, even
those closest to us will not understand. But this is the *right* way to
live, and that's the most important thing. However hard it gets,
whatever the battles or the ridicule, it remains the most important
thing.

Those supporting their gay friends have a countercultural role,
too. In this politically correct culture, just believing these things can
cause outrage among those who
do not agree. The biblical principles on which all of this stuff is
based are unpalatable to many.
But they are *true*, and this truth
needs to be communicated.

*... living according to
the Bible is about as
countercultural as
you can get.*

It is difficult for someone
like me to go out into the gay
community as an evangelist. It
would be like asking a recovering alcoholic to go out to be a
missionary in the bars and pubs
of London. My prayer is that,
now you can understand the issues better, you will be willing to be
a gospel witness to the gay community, loving them, getting
alongside them and pointing them to Christ; that you would desire
for God to bring more gay people into your life with whom to
have genuine friendships, not as 'projects' or 'targets', but as
people to love and share your Saviour with.

I cannot safely pray this for myself, so, if you are willing,
I would like you to pray something like the prayer below.

Imagine the impact this could have in God's kingdom!

Prayer

Lord, I understand that your gospel shows us that we have all fallen short of your standards, and so we are all in equally desperate need of a Saviour. Please keep my heart soft to this truth, so that I will be always willing to tell people the good news that can save them. Please especially open my eyes to see that this good news is applicable to everyone, even to those who seem far off, such as those in the gay community.

... this good news is applicable to everyone, even to those who seem far off, such as those in the gay community.

Lord, give me a particular burden for this group of people, so that many can be rescued and won for your kingdom. Please bring more gay people into my life, individually selected for me because we have a chance of a real and genuine friendship. Please help me to love those people well and with patience and compassion. Please bless me with opportunities and courage to tell them about you, so that they can know you too. Amen.

Suggestions for further reading

General reading

Jeanette Howard, *Out of Egypt* (London: Monarch Books, 2000)

Jeanette Howard, *Into the Promised Land* (Oxford: Monarch Books, 2005)

Martin Hallett, *Still Learning to Love* (The Wirral: How Publications, 2004)

Chapter 2: What the Bible says

Thomas E. Schmidt, *Straight and Narrow? Compassion and Clarity in the Homosexuality Debate* (Leicester: IVP, 1995)

Andrew Goddard, *Homosexuality and the Church of England* (Cambridge: Grove Books, 2004)

The appendix by Glenn N. Davies entitled 'Homosexuality in the New Testament', in Christopher Keane (ed.), *What Some of You Were: Stories about Christians and Homosexuality* (Australia: Matthias Media, 2001)

David Peterson (ed.), *Holiness and Sexuality: Homosexuality in a Biblical Context* (Milton Keynes: Paternoster Press, 2004)

For more on the Old Testament texts:

John Richardson, *What God Has Made Clean ... If We Can Eat Prawns, Why Is Gay Sex Wrong?* (MPA Books/The Good Book Company, 2003)

And for a different explanation of Old Testament application:
Marcus Honeysett, *Finding Joy: A Radical Rediscovery of Grace*
(Leicester: IVP, 2005)

Chapter 3: Origins
On the roots of homosexual orientation and on seeking healing
from God:
Andrew Comiskey, *Pursuing Sexual Wholeness – How Jesus Heals
the Homosexual* (Lake Mary, FL: Creation House, 1989)
Elizabeth R. Moberly, *Homosexuality: A New Christian Ethic*
(Cambridge: James Clarke & Co., 1983)

On the truth behind the gay propaganda:
Jeffrey Satinover, *Homosexuality and the Politics of Truth* (Grand
Rapids, MI: Baker Books, 1999)
Christopher Keane (ed.), *What Some of You Were* (Australia:
Matthias Media, 2001), Appendices 1 and 2

Chapter 4: Identity and evangelism
On identity:
Dan Sneed, *The Power of a New Identity* (Kent, England:
Sovereign World, 2000)
Dick Keyes, *Beyond Identity: Finding Your Self in the Image and
Character of God* (Ann Arbor, MI: Servant Books, 1984)
Briar Whitehead, *Craving for Love* (Tunbridge Wells: Monarch,
1993)

Chapter 5: After conversion
Al Hsu, *The Single Issue* (Leicester: IVP, 1998)
Christopher Keane (ed.), *What Some of You Were: Stories about
Christians and Homosexuality* (Australia: Matthias Media, 2001)

Chapter 6: Wrong reaction, right reaction
Lori Rentzel, *Emotional Dependency* (Leicester: IVP, 1990)

Notes

Chapter 2: What the Bible says

1 Quoted from an interview with Andy.

2 Whenever I talk about 'the church' in this book, I am referring to those evangelical churches that subscribe to the biblical viewpoint outlined in this chapter. It is important to note, however, that very large sections of the church do not hold this biblical view on the subject of homosexuality, but find it perfectly acceptable to condone homosexual conduct.

3 This section largely summarizes an excellent chapter entitled 'Sexuality from the Beginning', in Thomas E. Schmidt's *Straight and Narrow? Compassion & Clarity in the Homosexuality Debate* (Leicester: Inter-Varsity Press, 1995).

4 Once again, the 'Further reading' section (page 149) will assist those who wish to familiarize themselves with these passages.

Chapter 3: Origins

1 Excerpt from a conversation with Ruth.

2 There are differences between the causes of homosexuality in males and in females. There are also differences in the way that the struggles in sexuality manifest themselves. There is no space here to go into those differences; only to acknowledge that they exist.

3 For example, in a chapter called 'The Price of Love' in Thomas E. Schmidt, *Straight & Narrow?* (IVP, 1995), and in one called 'Is Homosexuality Desirable? Brute Facts' in Jeffrey Satinover, *Homosexuality and the Politics of Truth* (Baker Books, 1999).

4 For example: 'A significant majority of these men ... (69–83 percent) reported having 50 or more lifetime sexual partners, and over 80 percent had engaged in receptive anal intercourse with at least some of their partners in the previous two years',

R. A. Kaslow et al., 'The Multicentre AIDS Cohort Study: Rationale, Organization, and Selected Characteristics of the Participants', *American Journal of Epidemiology* 126, no. 2 (August 1987), pp. 310–318, as quoted in Jeffrey Satinover, *Homosexuality and the Politics of Truth* (Baker Books, 1999), p. 55. Or: 'consistent with the concentration of AIDS cases among high-risk populations, epidemiologists estimate that 30 percent of all twenty-year-old homosexual males will be HIV-positive or dead of AIDS by the time they are thirty', W. Odets, in a report to the American Association of Physicians for Human Rights, cited in E. L. Goldman, 'Psychological Factors Generate HIV Resurgence in Young Gay Men', *Clinical Psychiatry News* (October 1994), p. 5, and also quoted in Jeffrey Satinover, *Homosexuality and the Politics of Truth*, p. 57. There is a whole chapter full of such statistics and facts in Jeffrey Satinover's book.

5 For example, it has been known for radical feminists to have relationships with other women and to claim that this is because men are irrelevant, even for sex. In fact, some political homosexuals would have us believe that homosexuality is a choice for a much larger minority. While it is quite possible to believe that many could be seduced into the apparently liberating permissiveness of the gay scene as a whole (perhaps particularly for women, who might seek refuge in the aggressive security of separatism or feminism), I find it hard to believe that what makes a person sexually aroused can be 'chosen'. I can only believe that those who claim to have chosen to be gay are in fact acting on degrees of homosexuality already present in them which have yet, for whatever reason, gone unacknowledged. If sexuality were a matter of choice, the reverse would also be true: many Christians like me, struggling with unwanted homosexual feelings, could choose instead to be aroused by the opposite sex.

6 J. Bancroft, *British Journal of Psychiatry* 164 (1994), pp. 437–440.

7 For example: Glenn Wilson and Qazi Rahman, *Born Gay: The Psychobiology of Sex Orientation* (London: Peter Owen, 2005).

8   There are plenty of very helpful books available for anyone who wishes to research this area further. Please see the 'Further reading' section for details.

9   Byne et al., 'Human Sexual Orientation: The Biologic Theories Reappraised', *Archives of General Psychiatry* 50 (1993), pp. 228–239; and G. Vines, 'Obscure origins of desire', *New Scientist* 136 (1992), pp. 2–8; both quoted in Christopher Keane (ed.), *What Some of You Were* (Matthias Media, 2001), pp. 140–141.

10 It subsequently emerged that this was as a result of a systematic campaign on the part of the National Gay Task Force: Satinover, *Homosexuality and the Politics of Truth*, pp. 31–40.

11 E. V. Siegel, *Female Homosexuality: Choice Without Volition* (Hillsdale, NJ: The Analytic Press, 1988), p. xiii.

12 From an article in *The Guardian* on 28 June 2006 entitled 'Born Gay or Made Gay?'.

13 See the appendices at the back of *What Some of You Were*, edited by Christopher Keane, for more of these, or 'Homosexuality – the causes' pp. 19–28 in *Nucleus*, October 1997, by Rachael Pickering and Peter Saunders.

14 T. McGuire, *Journal of Homosexuality* 28 (1–2) (1995), pp. 115–145, quoted in 'Homosexuality – the causes', by Rachael Pickering and Peter Saunders.

15 L. Thompson, *TIME* Magazine, 12 June 1995, pp. 52–53, quoted in 'Homosexuality – the causes', by Rachael Pickering and Peter Saunders.

16 E. Eckert et al., *British Journal of Psychiatry* 148 (1986), pp. 421–425, quoted in 'Homosexuality – the causes', by Rachael Pickering and Peter Saunders.

17 Rachel Pickering and Peter Saunders, 'Homosexuality – the causes', *Nucleus* October (1977), pp. 19–28.

18 Dr Elizabeth Moberly's definition of healthy heterosexuality is 'the ability to relate healthily to *both* sexes'.

19 It is worth noting that it is possible that a person could be born with a genetic predisposition towards being vulnerable to the psychosocial factors: Vaughan Williams, 'Signposts to Wholeness',

Lecture 1 *Homosexuality: The Facts, Exploring the Nature Arguments*, examines this.

20 This is an over simplification for the sake of succinctness. Often these feelings are so deeply buried that the person will not even realize there is a problem with the same-sex parent.

21 From Jeanette Howard, *Out of Egypt: One Woman's Journey Out of Lesbianism* (London: Monarch, 2000), pp. 60–62.

22 From www.nspcc.org.uk in an article entitled 'Child Maltreatment in the United Kingdom: a study of the prevalence of child abuse and neglect'.

23 Living Waters is an evangelical healing programme that addresses sexual and relational brokenness. It is part of Desert Stream Ministries (www.desertstream.org).

24 From A. Comiskey, *Pursuing Sexual Wholeness – How Jesus Heals the Homosexual* (Lake Mary: Creation House, 1989), p. 133.

25 An excellent example is Living Waters (see note 23).

26 Author of *101 Frequently Asked Questions About Homosexuality* (Oregon: Harvest House, 2004) and manager of the Homosexuality and Gender Issues Department at Focus on the Family, as well as Chairman of the Board of Exodus International.

27 *101 Questions*, p. 132.

28 Ibid., p. 129.

29 Philippians 1:6.

Chapter 4: Identity and evangelism

1 Excerpt from an interview with Ella.

2 H. Brown, 'Themes in Experimental Research on Groups from the 1930s to the 1990s', in M. Wetherell (ed.), *Identities, Groups and Social Issues* (London: Sage/The Open University, 2002), p. 34.

3 I recognize that not all people with homosexual feelings will respond in the ways I describe in this chapter. Obviously I cannot represent all types of people, so I am choosing to represent the majority, to serve as a useful tool for Christians to consider in their witness.

4   Cartwright (1950), quoted in J. Crocker and D. M. Quinn, 'Psychological Consequences of Devalued Identities', in M. Brewer and M. Hewstone (eds), *Self and Social Identity* (Oxford: Blackwell, 2005), p. 440.

5   Daphna Oyserman, 'Self-Concept and Identity', in Brewer and Hewstone (eds), *Self and Social Identity*, p. 9.

6   V. Baird, *The No-Nonsense Guide to Sexual Diversity* (Oxford: New Internationalist, 2001), pp. 71–72.

7   M. A. Hogg, 'Social Categorization and Group Behaviour', in Brewer and Hewstone (eds), *Self and Social Identity*, p. 208.

8   I am not suggesting that these two scenarios are in fact parallel. One is a lifestyle issue, clearly condemned in the Bible. The other is the only true path to eternal life. This is simply an exercise to help us to get into the head of a gay person; to help us to see what that person *perceives* us as saying.

9   Homophobia is irrational hatred of people because of their sexuality.

Chapter 5: After conversion

1   Excerpt from an interview with Mark.

2   Excerpt from an interview with Ruth.

3   Rodney Clapp, *Families at the Crossroads* (Leicester: Inter-Varsity Press, 1993), p. 78.

4   The touch deficit is often exacerbated by the fact that defensive detachment has meant that many gay people have not been able to receive the touch they needed when they were growing up.

5   Al Hsu, *The Single Issue* (Leicester: IVP, 1998), pp. 47–48.

6   See Chapter 1.

Chapter 6: Wrong reaction, right reaction

1   Taken from an interview with Ruth. Ruth had a two-year relationship with Clare. Their relationship will act as the case study for the first half of this chapter.

2   From A. Comiskey, *Pursuing Sexual Wholeness – How Jesus Heals the Homosexual* (Lake Mary: Creation House, 1989), p. 133.

3 For example, look at the way Jesus balances speaking the truth with showing tenderness and compassion in speaking to the woman at the well (John 4:4–26); the woman caught in adultery (John 8:1–11); Zacchaeus (Luke 19:1–10); and Nicodemus (John 3:1–21). He is gentle, patient and compassionate with all of them, even though they are 'sinful' people.

4 The personal situations of both women are clearly much more complex than the way they are represented here. Both had their own histories and baggage, which will have informed their eventual choices and attitudes. It is not appropriate to go into all of these complexities in this chapter, but their stories do serve as a very useful case study to show the damaging effects of insensitivity from churches and Christian individuals.

5 Author of an amazingly helpful little booklet called *Emotional Dependency*, published by IVP.

6 From *Emotional Dependency* by Lori Rentzel (IVP, 1990), pp. 8–10.

7 Again borrowed from Lori Rentzel's booklet.

8 It is very important to make sure the roots of the problems are sought and addressed before God, if a break is taken. Otherwise it is likely that the friendship will lurch back into dependency, often even more powerfully than it did before, once the friends are reunited. A time apart without a real commitment to change can in fact sometimes do more harm than good. This does not mean that staying in the friendship is therefore the right thing to do; rather that seeking help is essential.

Chapter 7: Commissioning

1 Andrew Goddard, *Homosexuality and the Church of England* (Cambridge: Grove Books, 2004), p. 6 and quoting Stephen Fowl, *Engaging Scripture* (Oxford: Blackwell, 1998), pp. 121–122.